# The Healing of Satanically Ritually Abused Multiple Personality Disorder

## By

## John Clark, Ph. D

ISBN: 1-4107-1779-8 (e-book)
ISBN: 1-4107-1780-1 (Paperback)

Library of Congress Control Number: 2003090684


This book is printed on acid free paper.


Printed in the United States of America
Bloomington, IN

1stBooks – rev. 3/17/03

# TABLE OF CONTENTS

**Chapter Ten:**

# ACKNOWLEDGEMENTS

I want to thank my family for their love and patience while I was working with ritual abuse survivors.

I would also like to thank the Jim Smith for the opportunity to work with him for the past two years and the many opportunities to learn from him. He is truly a great brother in the Lord.

I also want to give thanks to the different survivors who were willing to relate their stories and experiences for this book and all of the ministries who supplied me with their individual research and insights.

Lastly, I want to give glory to Jesus Christ, for without Him, we can do nothing.

# INTRODUCTION

This book is about the healing of satanically ritually abused multiple personality disorder. "It is generally agreed that in about 97% of the cases where multiple personalities are formed, the victims suffered serious abuse at an early age, most of them have been abused sexually. They needed to use disassociation to cope with the abuse".[i] It is good to remember that in the healing is a process that most people who are S.R.A.M.P.D., the trauma happened at a very early age. II Corinthians 5:17 says, "Therefore if anyone is in Christ he is a new creation, the old is gone and the new is come"[ii], now the Greek reads, "Therefore if anyone is in Christ he is a new creation, the old is passing away and the new is coming". This speaks of a process of healing where the Lord takes someone who is S.R.A.M.P.D., who has been greatly abused and hurt, and takes them through their life circumstances and he heals them.

In the past two years, I have worked with S.R.A.M.P.D. for over 400 to 500 hours, and what I have learned through working with S.R.A's is that you cannot use a set formula. Everybody is different, every abuse is different and also, you can't depend totally on all the education you have because really, our total dependence on helping to put the personality back together and to help heal the hurting is on Jesus and the guiding of the Holy Spirit. I John 2:20 & 27, "But you have an anointing from the

Holy One and all of you know the truth", "As for you, the anointing you receive from Him remains in you and you do not need anyone to teach you but as this anointing teaches you about all things and as this anointing is real and not counterfeit just as it has taught you remain in Him".[iii] Education and training are just tools in the hands of the Master, tools that Jesus can use to help us in the hurting and the healing process. It is good to be educated, it is good to be learned, it is good to have psychological training, but we must depend on Jesus and the Holy Spirit to lead us, guide us, to reveal things to us that we need to know, and to help us see beyond what is seen to the unseen, as it relates to deliverance and healing for people who are S.R.A.M.P.D.

There will be a lot of things in this book that I will base on my own case study but there will be other things that I will base on what I have learned from other people. In fact, there are a lot of things that the Lord would like to teach us through other people. The scripture says as iron sharpens iron, so another man sharpens another man. It would be good before you read the rest of this book to read the chapter on the definition of terms so that as you read the book, you will understand the different terms being used.

I would ask the reader to have an open mind, the reason for this is that everything that I say and do in this book, I will base on what I see as a biblical view. But I know also, from working as a Pastor for nine years and as a hospital Chaplain for four years, that I have met people from many different denominations and many different walks of life, that have many different views on scripture, who have many different views on salvation, healing, deliverance, spiritual warfare, the gifts of the Holy Spirit, Satan, demons, and angels, etc. I will be dealing with all of these topics in this book. But, I believe that if we read the scripture, the scripture is very clear as it relates to salvation because the writer says in I John 5:13-15, "I write these things to you who believe in the name of the Son of God that you may know that you have eternal life and this is the confidence that we have in approaching God that if we ask anything according to His will he hears us and if we know that he hears us whatever we ask we know that we have what we ask of Him".iv Now in those short three verses the word know is used at least three times and the word confidence is used once and I believe from scripture you can know about salvation, you can know about healing, deliverance, warfare, the gifts of the Holy Spirit, Satan, demons, and angels, etc. You can know these things. God hasn't made it a mystery, He has made it plain so that you and I can be equipped to do battle against the forces of the darkness and win in Jesus' name.

My prayer is that as you read this book that you would be able to take the principals written in this book and use them in your life and ministry to help the hurting and the wounded and to help to set the captives free. This is my hearts cry, that God would not only use me but also, that those who read this book would be more equipped to help set the captives free. Isaiah 6:1-4, "The spirit of the sovereign Lord is on me because the Lord hath anointed me to preach good news to the poor He has set me to bind up the broken hearted to proclaim freedom for the captives and the release from darkness for the prisoners. To proclaim the year of the Lord's favor in the day of vengeance of our God to comfort all who mourn and to provide for those who grieve in Zion to bestow on them a crown of beauty instead of ashes, the oil of gladness instead of mourning, and a garment of praise instead of a spirit of despair, they will be called oaks of righteousness a planting of the Lord for the display of His splendor. They will rebuild the ancient ruins and restore places long devastated and they will renew the ruined cities that have been devastated for generations".[v] This is the exciting thing, as I see it, is that God desires to anoint just plain ordinary Christians, like myself, to go out and set the captives free. You don't have to be a super Christian to see people set free from the forces of darkness, you just have to be a vessel, willing to be used in the Master's hand. I Corinthians 1:27-31, "But God chose the foolish things of the world to shame the wise, God chose the weak things of the world to shame the strong, He chose the lowly things of this world and the despised things and the things that are not to nullify the things that are, so then no one may boast before Him, but it is because of Him that you are in Christ Jesus who has become for us the wisdom of God that is our righteousness, holiness, and redemption, therefore as it is written let him who boasts, boast in the Lord".[vi] You see, God wants to use normal people to do awesome, supernatural things for His kingdom. A lot of people look at people who are S.R.A.M.P.D. and they despise them, but God sees these people as a group of people that are hurting and wounded, and God doesn't see them as hurting and wounded, He sees them as warriors, He sees them as someone who He has died for, someone who He shed his blood for, someone who He wants to heal, and the good thing is, that God wants to use you and I to help build His kingdom and to take the land back from the enemy. Just another note to the reader, the 400 to 500 hours of case study with S.R.A.M.P.D., was a case study I did with a client who was being groomed for the World Council of the Satanic Church, the Council of Nine. Out of thirteen levels, the client was a nine in the satanic kingdom and the next step for this client would have been to be on the World Council and a lot of people said that this client was the only one they have ever known who was so high up in the satanic kingdom to get out. Not only to get out, but also to live to tell about it, and she came to our area. She came for protection, healing, and restoration. Her name will remain confidential. Some of the programming techniques, trauma, and things I'm going to talk about in this book, you may not have a lot of things to compare them with, even if you work with S.R.A.'s on a regular basis. But, some of the principals will be familiar to you. My prayer and hope through this book is that people would not only be equipped, but that they would be drawn closer to Jesus.

(All biblical quotations are from the N.I.V. Bible-Zondervan Publishing House).

# CHAPTER ONE

## THE BIBLICAL AND PSYCHOLGIAL
## UNDERSTANDING OF S.R.A.M.P.D.

In the beginning of this chapter I am putting two pictures first for the reader to look at, first is a picture of the personality the way God made it to be, tightly woven together, all in one piece and not frayed; the second picture is a picture of the personality, tightly woven at the bottom but frayed half way through, going all the way to the top. The dots on the frays are demonic spirits and the different frays are: core personalities, or core splits, and you'll see that as you look at the picture. You'll see which one is the host personality, you'll notice that core splits, will not have

1

memories back to the womb, you'll also notice the birth person in the middle, will have memories going all the way back to the womb. I'm putting these pictures at the beginning of the chapter so that the reader can refer back to them several times as a point of reference.

## A PERSONALITY
## THE WAY GOD CREATED

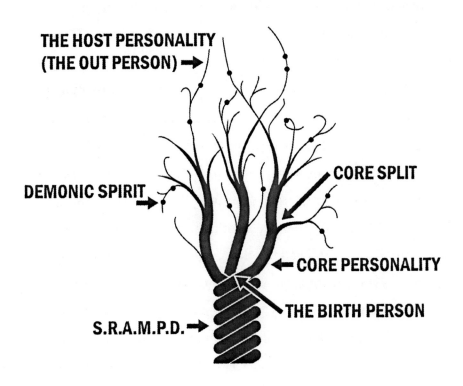

THE HOST PERSONALITY
(THE OUT PERSON) →

DEMONIC SPIRIT →

CORE SPLIT

← CORE PERSONALITY

← THE BIRTH PERSON

S.R.A.M.P.D. →

From the very beginning of the time when I became a Christian until now in my ministry, I've always been a person who is a firm believer, not only in God's power to save but also God's power to heal, physically, mentally and emotionally. I've also been a believer in people having demons and also been a believer in demons being cast out. Acts 5:12-16, "The apostles performed many miraculous signs and wonders amongst the people and all the believers used to meet together in Solomon's colonnade. No one else dared to join them even though they were highly regarded by the people, nevertheless more and more men and women believed in the Lord and were added to their number as a result the people brought their sick into the streets and laid them on beds and mats so that Peter's shadow might fall on some of them as he passed by. Crowds gathered also from the towns of Jerusalem bringing their sick and those tormented by evil spirits and all of them were healed".[vii] In this scripture, we see salvation going on, we see physical healing going on, and I believe we see mental healing going on at the same time. Although scripture doesn't go into great detail, scripture does let us know that the Lord's desire for us that we would be whole; spirit, soul, mind and body. I used to believe that multiple personalities were all demonic, even through Bible College up to my first four to five years of pastoral ministry. It seemed as though all the way through Bible College, I dealt with a lot of people who had demonic problems. Now that I look back, I believe that some of them were suffering from multiple personality disorder and other disorders. I was also a very firm believer back then, that all multiple personalities and voices in the head were demonic problems, I see now that this is not the case. Some of it may have been demonic problems, but some of it was the personalities themselves. The other dilemma that I ran into as I thought about multiple personalities and multiple personality disorder was that, how can someone who is a Christian still have a demon? It doesn't fit the normal, traditional Christian beliefs. How can the Holy Spirit and the demonic spirit dwell in the same vessel at the same time? I remember on a Sunday, I had a lady come to my church who had accepted Jesus Christ into her heart a couple of weeks earlier. She came up front and said, "Pastor, would you pray for me? I'm hearing voices in my head and I would like prayer." So, I said, "I won't pray for you by myself, but I will pray with you with my prayer team". At this time I was pastoring in the Wesleyan Denomination, and so we got her in the back room and we had about five other people on the prayer team, and we began to pray, and as we prayed she said, "You know you're really not getting anywhere", I said, "In the name of the Lord, Jesus Christ, I command this blockage to be removed", when I did that, she just about shot straight up off her chair and a growling voice came out of her mouth and this demon began speaking to me. At that time in my ministry, I was in my first or second year of pastoral ministry, I had never dealt with such a situation, but we began to pray and bind this demonic spirit in the name Jesus. After about an hour of prayer and commanding, two

5

demonic spirits left and the young lady opened her eyes and I said, "Are you okay?" and she said, "Yes", and I said, "Do you have anymore voices in your head?" and she said, "No, My mind is clear". I left that meeting not only giving glory to God but thinking, how can this be, how can someone who is a born again Christian, who has repented, accepted Christ into their heart, still have a demon? And then I remember one day I was reading a book by John Wimber called "Power Healing" and in this book he said, "The correct word is not oppression or possession, the correct word is demonized. That people are demonized to the extent that they have opened their lives and hearts to the enemy is the extent that the enemy is allowed to have a foothold to control their lives".[viii] As I began to think about that, it began to make a whole lot of sense and I began to understand how, yes truly, one could be born again and still have demonic problems; if those areas where the demonic has had the legal right to have the foothold have not been dealt with. We saw earlier in II Corinthians 5:17 the Greek translation of that verse is, "If anyone be in Christ he is a new creation, the old is passing away and the new is coming". We see that healing is a process, and deliverance is a process. we also know from our studying the scripture that sanctification, being sanctified until we are set apart for God, is also a process. But even though I realized this about demonization and how a Christian could have a demon, I still was not a believer in multiple personality disorder in my first four years of pastoral ministry.

It wasn't until about our fifth year in ministry in pastoring a church that we had a lady visit our church, this was after we had left the Wesleyan Denomination and went into the Assembly of God, when we had a revival going on. I knew this lady; I knew there was something different about her because she acted in ways that I had not seen before. Up to this time, I had not really dealt with a lot of Satanists; I had dealt with only a few people who had been in the Satanic Occult. I knew she had been a Satanist and that there was really something different about her. She ended up being a client that I began working with about a year later, helping her in the healing process, healing from multiple personality disorder. I remember the way I got involved with this. If you would have told me about seven years ago that I would be involved with helping people get out of the occult and helping people who have multiple personality disorder come into healing, I would have told you that you were nuts. But, one day I remember I was sitting down reading my Bible and actually, it was a day I was in prayer, and we'll call this lady S.R.A. #1, and God gave me a word, that even though she was frayed and torn apart, He was going to put her back one fray at a time. He was going to take the broken pieces of her life and put her back together until she was whole. I remember that as I was writing this down, I really felt I had a word for her that the Lord wanted me to give her. I had been reading a scripture and God began to shine the light of His Spirit upon me and give me revelation about multiple personality disorder. The scripture is found in Psalm

7

139:1-24, "Oh Lord you have searched me and you know me. You know when I set and when I rise, you perceive my thoughts from afar, you discern my going out and my lying down, you are familiar with all my ways. Before a word is on my tongue you know it completely oh Lord. You hem me in behind and before, you have laid your hand upon me. Such knowledge is too wonderful for me, too lofty for me to attain, where can I go from your spirit, and where can I flee from your presence. If I go up to the heavens you are there, if I make my bed in the depths you are there. If I rise on the wings of the dawn, and if I settle on the far side of the sea, even there your hand will guide me, your right hand will hold me fast. If I say surely the darkness will hide me and the light become night around me, even the darkness will not be dark to you, the night will shine like the day for darkness is as light to you. For you created my inmost being, you knit me together in my mother's womb. I praise you because I am fearfully and wonderfully made and your works are wonderful, I know that full well. My frame was not hidden from you when I was made in the secret place. When I was woven together in the depths of the earth, your eyes saw my unformed body. All the days ordained for me are written in your book before one of them came to be. How precious to me are your thoughts oh God, how vast is the sum of them, were I to count them they would outnumber the grains of the sand. When I awake I am still with you. If you only would slay the wicked, oh God, away from me you bloodthirsty men. They speak of you with evil intent. Your adversaries misuse your name. I do not hate those who hate you oh Lord, and abhor those who rise up against you. Have I nothing but hatred for them, I count them my enemies. Search me oh God and know my heart, test me and know my anxious thoughts, see if there be any offensive way in me and lead in the way of everlasting".[ix] As I began to read this scripture, the Lord began to bring me revelation and understanding about multiple personality disorder. He began to show me the words in this scripture in verse 13 that was used, the words are "you knit" and "woven together". In my mind's eye the Lord gave me a picture of a piece of rope, the first piece of rope was like a normal piece of rope that you would buy out of a store and the Lord kind of asked me the question in my spirit, "How many pieces of rope do you have in your hand?" I remember I thought, well I only had one piece of rope. The Lord said, "Think again, look at that rope, you have many different strands of rope, tightly knit and woven together in one piece". Then the Lord began to show me what a multiple personality was, that through trauma and through abuse, Satan tries to pull the strands back away from the core. He then hooks demons to the strands, so you have a mixture of the personality and you have a mixture of the demonic. This is where I began to get my understanding of what a multiple personality was and I remember that I called that lady on the phone all excited, I had the word for her and I began to share with her what God had revealed to me She then asked me to be one of the care givers that would help her in the healing process.

Not knowing what I was getting into, not knowing any of the experiences that I would be having, just having a basic understanding of how God made the personality, tightly woven together and yet how the enemy tries to split and fray back the personality, to the point where there are several multiple personalities with demons hooked to them, I said yes. So that is where I got my basic understanding of what I feel is the Biblical understanding of M.P.D. Then the Lord showed me the way the personalities are healed. First of all, every alter personality must first accept Jesus; secondly, the demons must be removed from the personality; thirdly, truth must be faced, this is where Jesus takes them back and shows them the truth about how they were split, and how they were hurt, and He brings healing; fourthly, vows must be broken; fifthly, only Jesus can integrate them to the place where he intended them to be from the very beginning; and sixth, all this must be the free will and free choice of the alter being dealt with. Then wherever the Lord integrates them back into whatever alter they were split from, that alter must learn to cope with the different memories that are remembered after the integration happens. It's kind of like a circuit, when the personality is frayed from the core, the circuit is broken and the alter cannot remember the memories, but after an alter integrates into another alter, the memories become reconnected and can be remembered and so there tends to be, at this point, a lot of psychological counseling that needs to be done. So we see that multiple personality disorder is a two-fold problem. First of all, it's a psychological problem and second, it's a spiritual problem. So, if we just treat the psychological side of it, you can't truly bring healing to someone who has S.R.A.M.P.D. because you not only have to treat the psychological part of it, you also have to treat the spiritual part of it in order to bring healing to someone who has been deeply traumatized through satanic ritual abuse and who also has multiple personality disorder. I will go more in depth in the healing of multiple personality disorder further on in this book but truly one thing I have learned over the course of time is that, when dealing with someone who has multiple personality disorder, the team who is dealing with them, you really are dependent not only on Jesus and the Holy Spirit, but you are dependent on the different gifts and abilities God has given different people to bring healing in a person's life. It really is the ministry of the body to those that are hurting and wounded, not just the ministry of one individual. As we bring our gifts and abilities together, God can use us to help heal the hurting and wounded. II Corinthians 10:4-5 says, "The weapons we fight with are not weapons of the world, on the contrary, they have divine power to demolish strongholds. We demolish arguments and every pretension that sets itself up against the knowledge of God and we take every thought captive and make it obedient to Christ".[x] In dealing with S.R.A.M.P.D., we are truly dependent not only on our psychological training but also on the divine weapons that God has given us to demolish the strongholds of the enemy in a person's life and bring wholeness and healing to an

11

individual. Then when you bring people together in the body of Christ, and they bring their divine weapons and you bring your divine weapons, you can truly team up to bring deliverance and healing in people's lives. I want to thank the Lord for my opportunity to work with The Jim Smith. We teamed up together for one year and worked side by side for over 400 hours with S.R.A.M.P.D. The value of working together, and bringing your gifts and abilities together to help in a person's healing is very valuable and important.

In the past three years, it has been my privilege as I worked with S.R.A.M.P.D. to work with Cheryl S. Night and Jo M. Getzinger, on occasions at C.A.R.E. Ministries. They have done extensive work in the area of S.R.A.M.P.D. and they have written a great book called "Care Giving, The Cornerstone of Healing". In this book they talk about what multiple personality disorder is and what satanic ritual abuse is. "Multiple personality disorder or otherwise known as M.P.D., is perhaps the most creative, intelligent, elegant coping mechanism and survival technique humans are capable of creating. The foundation of M.P.D. is disassociation, a psychological response that enables a person to block especially horrible experiences such as child abuse, from her memory. According to Frank Putman, a psychiatrist at the National Institute of Mental Health, and the leading expert in the field of multiplicity, M.P.D., have its origin in children before the age of 10 or 12, usually as a result of the worst kind of physical, sexual, emotional and mental abuse and often a preverbal child before age 5. At a point when the abuse exceeds a child's ability to accept it into its consciousness, some children simply say this is not happening. But of course it is happening, so in the beginning of this incredibly complex process, the child creates another personality to absorb the pain and terror that threaten to overwhelm the core personality, or birth person (the ability to hand) off this pain and torture to an alter personality helps. (The child survives). As the abuse continues especially in the case of ritualistic or satanic abuse more personalities may be created to take the torment. In the case of satanic ritual abuse the occult perpetrators may actually introduce further fragmenting of the personalities system by creating cult split. This newly created alter personality often called satanic, ritual or evil, is generally programmed to adhere to cult ideology without question".

"Over time the child's alter personalities may become more complete and to some extent autonomous, often having major responsibilities such as performing the core personality's daily work...(What began as a survival mechanism often becomes a stumbling block for those with M.P.D. and may even prevent them from leading a healthy, functional life". For instance, at the first of even routine stress, the alters can take over or switch in an effort to deal with a problem and protect the core personality; however, the core personality never learns to deal with pain, disappointment, fear and other crises of daily life". [xi]

What is satanic ritual abuse? Ritual abuse is any systematic pattern or practice by an individual or a group toward children

13

(or adults who are emotionally and or physically unable to resist or escape) that constitutes abuse of power in order to harm and control the victim. Such practices may sometimes appeal to some higher authority or power and justification of the action taken. This abuse may be mental, physical, emotional, spiritual or sexual.

Ritual abuse is aimed at deepening the silence of the already powerless, the poor, the young, the innocent, the used, and the desperate. Victims are often forced to engage in promiscuous or sadistic acts, sacrifices in which one or more persons may be tortured and killed, cannibalism, pornography, drug abuse and other provocative and cruel abuses. Societies denial of ritual abuse must be recognized as an enabling stance that assists in the continued perpetration of these heinous acts. "1) Ritual abuse is about secrecy, power and total control. 2) Ritual abuse is torture. It is a calculated effort on the part of perpetrators to systematically brainwash victims through physical, emotional, sexual and spiritual violation. 3) Perpetrators attempt to destroy basic human values and inculcate their own distorted belief systems. Through the use of mental coercion and physical torture they are able to gain control of a victim's thought process and behavior. 4) There is an attempt to distort a victim's sense of self and reality so that he or she feels personally responsible for the heinous acts of violence, which are being committed. 5) The child/victim is trained to make and enact violent decisions and to believe that the desire to behave that way comes out of their own innate evil. Therefore victims are often unable to hold their perpetrators responsible. 6) Many cult rituals violate state and or national laws. Abuse can include promiscuous and or sadistic acts, sacrifices, cannibalism and other provocative and cruel abuses. 7) Ritualistic crimes are generally motivated by the perpetrators' desire to control and abuse the victim. Any ideology can be used as a justification or a framework for abuse. 8) Often victims are programmed to kill themselves if they ever reveal information about specific rituals and or the organizational structure and leadership within the cult".

"Satanic ritual abuse is very different from normal child abuse in that the abusers are not merely acting out their own sickness or unresolved rage from their own childhood abuse. Cult abusers are following a prescribed ways of preparing children for cult membership and receptivity to Satan's demands. The following goals of ritual abuse are conscious and distinguish it from more commonly recognized child abuse. First of all ritual abuse specifically promotes certain forms of dissociation which will result in splitting or fragmentation of self-identity. This increases susceptibility to cult control and is believed to foster astral projection (out of body experiences), which is an important ability to develop in the cult. Second, ritual abuse targets the elimination of all spontaneous emotional feelings or even a unique sense of self. Basically the cult wants to create "robots" to be programmed and directed according to cult rules and purposes. Emotions are only to be elicited at the convenience of the cult in

15

service of certain tasks or learning's. Third, ritual abuse purposefully interferes with important early development processes such as object constancy and promotes a perpetual fear of abandonment. The cult intervenes often with infants and toddlers to destroy basic attachments (switching mother figures), which would normally promote internal security. Fourth, ritual abuse ensures the longevity of the cult by utilizing brainwashing techniques resulting in periods of amnesia for cult involvement while guaranteeing cult control. Free will has no place in orthodox Satanism, and the cult does not allow members to leave without significant retaliation".

In this chapter I have attempted to present a biblical understanding and a psychological understanding of S.R.A.M.P.D. There still is a whole lot to learn but I believe God has given us a basic understanding of how S.R.A.M.P.D. works. Enough understanding to be able to minister to these people by faith and allow God to use our spiritual and psychological training and bring it all together, mix it with the divine weapons of our warfare to see people who are S.R.A.M.P.D. healed, set free, totally integrated, back together, whole and set in their place in the body of Christ.

# CHAPTER TWO

## SEVENTEEN PRINCIPALS OF SPIRITUAL WARFARE BASED ON GOD'S WORD

We will discuss the principals of spiritual warfare based on God's word that in my 400 to 500 hours of case study with S.R.A.M.P.D., we were able to use these spiritual principals. They were very key in helping those who had come out of the satanic cult and those that wanted to come into healing, these spiritual principals of warfare really made the difference between victory and defeat, as it relates to breaking satanic programming and the satanic strongholds that the enemy had in people's lives. The following is not an exhaustive list of principals but are just

17

some of the basic spiritual principals and scriptures that we were able to use in session work and in the healing process for those that were survivors of satanic ritual abuse. Hebrews 4:12-13 says, "For the word of God is living and active. Sharper than any double edged sword it penetrates even to the dividing of soul and spirits, bone and marrow. It judges the thoughts and attitude of the heart. Nothing in all creation is hidden from God's sight everything is uncovered and laid bare before the eyes of Him to whom we must give an account".[xii3] So we see that the word of God is one of the most powerful weapons that can be used and one of the most powerful tools that we have when biblically counseling and helping survivors of satanic ritual abuse come in to healing.

Principal #1) We are in a spiritual battle. Whether people like to admit it or not, we are at war with the kingdom of darkness. The kingdom of darkness is fighting against the kingdom of light. As Christians, we cannot afford to sit idly by on the sidelines, as people are becoming casualties of the kingdom of darkness. Ephesians 6:10-18 says, "Finally be strong in the Lord and in his mighty power. Put on the full armor of God so you can take your stand against the devil's schemes. For our struggle is not against flesh and blood but against the rulers, against the authorities, against the powers of this dark world and against the spiritual forces of evil in the heavenly realms. Therefore, put on the full armor of God so that when the day of evil comes you will be able to stand your ground after you have done everything to stand,

stand. Stand firm then with the belt of truth buckled around your waist, with the breastplate of righteousness in place and with your feet fitted with a readiness that comes from the gospel of peace. In addition of this take up the shield of faith with which you can extinguish all the flaming arrows of the evil one. Take the helmet of salvation and the sword of the spirit, which is the word of God. Pray in the spirit on all occasions with all kinds of prayers and requests. With this in mind be alert and always be praying for all the saints".[xiii][4] "The theme of the principalities and the powers of the air is foundational to all true seeing. The remarkable thing, though, is that it has to do with something totally invisible there is a whole realm of invisible, angelic spirit entities that have a profound influence over the conduct and course of individuals and nations. This topic is both difficult and complex in every way. It is difficult because it is unfamiliar to us and complex because it is strenuously opposed by the powers of darkness. How negative, ignorant and indifferent the church is toward the powers of darkness, despite the fact that this theme is absolutely foundational to the whole calling of the church it is a perspective that pertains to the whole reality and of what God is about. The church has characteristically majored in the minors and has ignored this major theme. All of our activity therefore is condemned to a certain of futility and fruitlessness. We dissipate our energy always and walk on a horizontal level and in an earthly way. Paul reminds us that we wrestle not against flesh and blood".

The reason that this is such foundational principal when dealing with S.R.A.M.P.D. and people who are survivors of satanic ritual abuse is because you cannot deal with satanic ritual abuse and multiple personality disorder without having not only to deal with the human part of the personality, but also with the demons that are also involved; because in the programming of S.R.A.M.P.D., the cult purposely puts in demons and hooks demons to the different parts of personality. So, we are at war. This is a spiritual battle and the enemy is playing for keeps. John 10:10 says, "The thief comes only to steal and kill and destroy, I have come that they may have life and have it to the full". People in Satanism worship Satan just as seriously as Christians worship the Lord God Almighty. So as we found as we worked with people who are S.R.A.M.P.D., we had to not only deal with the human reality, but we also had to deal with the reality that we would have to deal with principalities, powers and demonic forces. Praise God we have been given the victory. The problem is that in the church today there is a lot of dispute on this subject. Many churches hardly believe in a real devil and demons, a lot of them don't believe in it at all, and, a lot of churches like to ignore spiritual warfare as if it doesn't exist. Just because we ignore spiritual warfare doesn't mean that it's going to go away. When survivors of satanic ritual abuse are coming into healing, we are literally taking people from the kingdom of darkness and bringing them into the kingdom of light. We can be assured that the enemy is not going to give up ground without a fight.

Principal #2) Jesus came to destroy the devil's works. I John 3:8 says, "He who does what is sinful is of the devil because the devil has them sinning from the beginning. The reason the Son of God appeared was to destroy the devil's works". "Then war broke out in heaven Michael and his angels going forth to battle with the dragon and the dragon and the angels fought and they were defeated and there was no more room found for them in heaven any longer. (Revelations 12:7-8 Amplified version) Note the phrase, there was no room for them in heaven. The war against the principalities involved displacement. Christ filling the spiritual territories once held by Satan". As we work with people that need deliverance, we must realize the very reason the Son of God came to earth was to destroy the devil's works. So when we work with people who are wounded, who are hurting, who are survivors of satanic ritual abuse and who have multiple personalities, we also realize that one of the basic foundational principals is this, that as they come into healing, the demonic strongholds, the demonic ground that has been held, is destroyed by the work of Jesus, this is Jesus' work not ours. It is not us crushing the forces of darkness, it is the Lord destroying the enemy and his demons, setting the captives free and bringing people into healing. Principal #3) There is only one true foundation. I Peter 2:7-8 says, "Now to you who believe this stone is precious but to those who do not believe the stone the builders rejected as become the capstone and a stone that causes men to stumble and a rock that makes them fall. They stumble because

21

they disobey the message which is also what they were destined for". One of the things we see when dealing with Satanism is that people that are truly involved with worshipping Satan really believe that they have the one true foundation that they are standing on and they believe it so much that they are willing to test their foundation against the word of God. As we know from the scripture that Jesus is the capstone, He is the cornerstone of the foundation that we stand on and those that fall against Him get crushed and any false foundation that comes against the one true foundation will be seen for exactly what it is, false, because the only true foundation there is, is the foundation of Jesus Christ. This is powerful when you help survivors of satanic ritual abuse come into healing, once they see that everything that they were told is a lie and false, it is much easier to help them come into healing and wholeness in Jesus Christ. Principal #4) Humility is key to victory in the battle. Psalms 149:4 says, "For the Lord takes the delight in his people he crowns the humble with salvation". We see from this scripture that God gives the victory to the humble. We must realize when we deal with healing and when we deal with tearing down the strongholds of the enemy, that humility is key to the battle. If we get arrogant, prideful and think that in our own power and our education we are winning such a great battle in seeing these people come into healing, we are really on the verge of suffering a major defeat. "To my amazement, when the arrows of pride struck the warriors they did not even notice. However, the enemy kept shooting, the warriors were bleeding, and getting weaker fast but they would not acknowledge it. Soon they were too weak to hold up their shields and swords, they cast them down declaring that they no longer needed them. They started taking off the armor, saying it is not needed anymore either, then another enemy division appeared and moved up swiftly. It was called strong delusion. Its members released a hail of arrows and they all seemed to hit the mark. Just a few of the demons of delusion, which were all small and seemingly weak, led away this once great army of glorious warriors. They were all taken to different prison camps, each named after the different doctrine of demons. I was astounded at how this great company of the righteous had been so easily defeated, and they still did not know what had hit them. I blurted out, how could those who were so strong who have been all the way to the top of the mountain, who have seen the Lord as they have, been so vulnerable? Pride is the hardest enemy to see and it always sneaks up behind you. In some ways those who have been at the greatest heights are in the greatest danger of falling. You must always remember that in life you can fall at any time from any level. Take heed when you think you stand lest you fall". So it is good to remember that when we are in the battle and helping people to come into healing, that we must constantly be reminded to cloak ourselves with the mantle of humility. Principal #5) Fasting and prayer are essential to the pulling down of the enemy's strongholds. "Whenever our church sends out a young minister to plan a new church in another community, we ask that his first action be to fast for at least 10 days. Fasting will help fine-tune his spiritual senses making it easy for him to identify any of Satan's strongholds in the city, including leviathan. Fasting seems to sensitize his discernment, helping him to understand the devil's principalities and territorial spirits in the area. Once recognized, these young usurping, evil beings can be dealt with powerfully. You can't deal with the enemy you don't recognize. Satan's work is under cover. It is secretive, deceptive and hidden. That is why fasting is so crucial to the beginning a new work in a city or community. We have learned that ministers who have fasted first become successful and fruitful quickly. But those who bypass this step seem to struggle with the same problems year after year". When helping people come into healing it is essential that people fast and pray because as Dave Williams just said, when you fast and pray it helps to fine tune our senses. In a lot of the satanic programming the satanic plans and schemes, and strongholds in a person's life are invisible. The only way to see these things and to have these things identified is that if we spend time with Jesus and we begin fasting and praying, and asking the Holy Spirit to reveal to our minds the things that we need to see. Matthew 17:21, "But this kind does not go out except by prayer and fasting". In this scripture, a demon possessed boy is brought to the disciples and the disciples could not cast the demon out and Jesus told them that it was not only because of their lack of faith, but it was because they hadn't fasted and prayed before dealing with that spirit. We see as we deal with demonic programming, the demonic realm and with helping a multiple come into wholeness, these are the things we really need the Lord's help on. There are some things that we are going to deal with that we will only be able to overcome by prayer and fasting. Principal #6) Be sure to inquire of the Lord. Joshua 9:14-15, "The men of Israel sampled the provisions but did not inquire of the Lord. Then Joshua made a treaty of peace with them and let them live and the leaders of the assembly ratified it by oath". In this story we see that the Gibeonites, who were really enemies of Israel, were very afraid of Israel and said if we don't do something, Israel is going to attack us and kill us. So they pretended that they were worshippers of God, that they had traveled from afar and that they had come to worship the Lord, God of Israel. Well, what they did was took some old moldy bread and their water bottles that were all empty, and they marched up to Joshua and the children of Israel and said that they had come from afar and that they had come to worship God. The major mistake that Joshua made that day is that he did not inquire of the Lord. He did not seek the Lord's guidance and direction as to what he should do with Gibeonite people; so Joshua ended up making a treaty of peace with them to let them live. The point is this, when you are dealing with the powers of darkness, with satanic programming or dealing with so much trauma, hurt and woundedness, we need to be inquiring of the Lord. We need to be getting guidance from God to know what to do and what not to do. Also, one needs to pray, "does God really want me working with people who are S.R.A.M.P.D. and is this God's plan?" Let me tell you why this is important, one of the things that the cult will do, one of the ploys that they have, is that when a ministry or a minister is doing a great work for God, they will send someone who is S.R.A.M.P.D. into the church seeking help. The whole plan is to get that pastor and that ministry so distracted from the work of the ministry, that they quit doing the one thing that God wants them to do and they begin to focus all their time and energy in another area. That is why it is so important that as we are helping survivors come into healing, as we are dealing with traumatic situations in multiple personalities, that we seek God's direction daily. That we seek his direction every time before we go into session, so that we know what to do and what not to do. Principal #7) The unseen world is more real than the physical world. II Corinthians 4:18, "So we fix our eyes not on what is seen but on what is unseen. For what is seen is temporary and what is unseen is eternal". This is very important to understand when we deal with multiple personalities and the unseen world. The unseen world is truly a reality and actually is more real than the physical world we live in. Principal #8) Jesus disarmed the principalities and powers of darkness. Colossians 2:14-15, "Having cancelled the written code with its regulations that was against us and that stood opposed to us He took it away by nailing it to the cross. And having disarmed the powers and authorities He made a public spectacle of them triumphing over them by the cross". This is one of the things I want to stress here

26

at this point, it is one thing to read the scripture and know it, but it is another thing to really believe it in your heart. The Bible says without faith it is impossible to please God. So when you are dealing with physical realities, psychological realities, and spiritual realities that are at work in the world around us, we must understand and believe these things, not only from our head but also from our heart. I praise God for this one fact that Jesus has totally disarmed the powers and authority. When Jesus Christ died on the cross he went down into hell, he took the keys of death, hell, and the grave from the devil and he rose victorious from the grave over him. He disarmed the enemy and the forces of darkness. So when dealing with S.R.A.M.P.D. and a spirit comes up or a demonic force comes up, we can stand strong in the name of Jesus, knowing that if we are born again believers and we have Christ in our hearts and the Holy Spirit lives in us, that we are covered with the blood of Jesus and we are armed with his authority and with his authority, there isn't any demonic force or spirit that can stand up against us. Principal #9) We must test every spirit. I John 4:1, "Dear friends do not believe every spirit, but test the spirits to see whether they are from God, because many false prophets have gone out into the world". In this scripture where the Bible tells us to test the spirits to see whether they be from God, it's not just talking demonic spirits but also talking about human spirits. I have found this specifically helpful when dealing with multiple personality disorder, when we deal with someone that has been ritually abused, it is good always

27

when another personality comes out, to test that spirit to see whether that spirit is from God. One of the things we found helpful in testing the spirits is this, when a multiple comes out and says, "I'm a part of the personality and my name is so and so", we would often tell them "Look we need to do a test here, and if you are truly a part of the personality, we don't want to hurt you or to insult you" then we would say, "In the name of Jesus Christ who came in the flesh, the Son of God, are you human or are you demon?" and we would wait for the answer. Demons would never say they were human. One of the things we would have them do is confess that Jesus Christ is Lord, and the scripture says that no one can say Jesus Christ is Lord except by the Holy Spirit. So, it is good to test the spirits because first of all, demons are liars, they never tell the truth. Therefore, if you wind up talking to a demon, he might really try to mislead you in the healing process, and so on and so forth. So, it is always good that we test the spirits. Principal #10) Jesus delegated his authority to us. Matthew 28:18-20, "And Jesus came to them all authority in heaven and in earth has been given to me therefore go and make disciples of all nations baptizing them in the name of Father, and of the Son and of the Holy Spirit and teaching them to obey everything I have commanded you and surely I am always with you to the very end of the age". Luke 9:1-2, "When Jesus had called the twelve together He gave them power and authority to drive out all demons and to cure diseases and He sent them out to preach the kingdom of God and to heal the sick". Luke 10:1, 8-

11, "After this the Lord appointed seventy two others and sent them two by two ahead of Him to every place where he was about to go. When you enter a town and are welcome eat what is set before you, heal the sick that are there and tell them the kingdom of God is near. But when you enter a town and are not welcome go into the streets and say even the dust of that town sticks to our feet we wipe off against you yet be sure of this the kingdom of God is near". It is good to remember and understand that the same authority that Jesus carried, and the same authority that he delegated to his disciples, he has delegated to us. He has given us the mission to teach, preach, heal the sick and deliver those who are bound by demonic oppression. The book of Acts is still being written, it is still going on. Malachi 3:6, "I the Lord do not change so you oh descendents of Jacob are not destroyed". I'm so happy and glad to know that God does not change and the Bible says that Jesus Christ is the same yesterday, today and forever, therefore the way he worked in the book of Acts, he's still working today. We can be armed, we can be equipped with the same power and the same authority that Jesus and his disciples had. We can have the same success they had in the book of Acts. This gives real hope. We do not stand in human authority, we do not stand in the authority of just a man, we stand in the authority of Jesus Christ, the Son of God, who came in the flesh, crucified, buried and then the third day rose victoriously over the grave and now lives in us by the Holy Spirit. We have that same power, that same resurrection life and power flowing through our veins. We walk in the authority that Jesus Christ has delegated to us and this is key to helping survivors of satanically ritually abused and those that who have multiple personality disorder come into healing. If you go into this work and you don't know who you are in Christ and don't know your authority, you won't be a success. Principal #11) It is by His spirit. Zechariah 4:6, "So he said to me this is the word of the Lord to Zerubbabel not by might, nor by power, but by My spirit saith the Lord Almighty". When we are dealing with the forces of darkness and putting the personality back together, it is important to remember, that we are not doing this in human might or in human wisdom, we are doing this in the might of the Holy Spirit whom God has given us, and by the wisdom and revelation that the Lord brings to us as we are working in counseling session and with those who are survivors. Principal #12) The battle must be fought with God's spiritual weapons. II Corinthians 10:4-5, "The weapons we fight with are not weapons of the world. On the contrary, they have divine power to demolish strongholds. We demolish arguments and every pretension that sets itself up against the knowledge of God, and we take captive every thought and make it obedient to Christ". It's important to remember that as we deal with the spiritual battle, the spiritual forces, and the heavenly realms, that the weapons that we fight with are not of the world. Some of the weapons are as follows: the sword of the spirit, when Jesus was being tempted by the enemy in the wilderness for 40 days and 40 nights, one of the things you read in Matthew 4:1-11, you hear

Jesus say constantly is, "it is written", "it is written", "it is written". The sword of the spirit, which is the word of God, is one of the most powerful weapons. The next weapon we fight with is prayer, getting down on our knees and praying. The next weapon is the blood of Jesus. The blood of Jesus is stronger than any weapon in the world; because it's by the blood of Jesus we have gained victory. The next weapon would be the name of Jesus. Acts 16:16-18, "Once when they were going to the place of prayer they were met by a slave girl that had a spirit by which she predicted the future. She earned a great deal for her owners by fortune telling. This girl followed Paul and the rest of us shouting "These men are servants of the Most High God who are telling you the way to be saved", she kept this up for many days finally, Paul became so troubled that he turned around to the spirit, "In the name of Jesus Christ, I command you to come out of her" and at that moment the spirit left her". We see in this scripture, the great power in the name of Jesus. The next weapon we can use is the gifts of the Holy Spirit. In I Corinthians 12:12-14, we see the different gifts of the Holy Spirit that are mentioned. I am not going to mention all of them but I will mention some of them. They would be prophesy, tongues, interpretation of tongues, gifts of healing, gifts of faith, word of wisdom, word of knowledge, working of miracles, and so on and so forth. I realize that a lot of people today, and lot of churches, believe that the gifts of the Holy Spirit passed away when the twelve apostles died, but the book of Acts is still being written, the gifts of the Spirit are still in

31

operation today.  They never passed away, they've always been around even through church history, and it is so important that we use the gifts of the Holy Spirit in the healing process.  When we don't know what to do, God can give us a word of wisdom or a word of knowledge, when healing is needed, God can funnel a gift of healing through us so that the person might receive healing.  So the gifts of the Holy Spirit, they are essential weapons in winning the battle.  Another important factor in the battle is that we should always be clothed with the full armor of God.  The Bible says in Ephesians 6:13, "Put all the full armor of God so that when the day of evil comes you may be able to stand your ground after that you have done everything to stand" It's important that we put on the belt of truth, the helmet of salvation, and the breastplate of righteousness, that our feet are fitted with readiness that comes from the gospel of peace and that we take up the shield of faith, the sword of the spirit which is the word of God, and that we pray in the spirit on all occasions of prayers and requests and that we stay alert and we pray for all the saints.  This is so crucial in winning the battle.  Principal #13) The anointing breaks the yoke.  Isaiah 10:27, "And it shall come to pass in that day that his burden shall be taken away from off thy shoulder, and his yoke from off thy neck, and the yoke shall be destroyed because of the anointing".  It is very important to understand and to realize that it is the anointing that breaks the yoke.  It's the anointing that sets people free from the powers of darkness. It's the anointing that enables someone who is very wounded, and who has memories that they can't get away from, to be healed. It's the anointing that can take someone who has multiple personalities and bring him or her back together. Everything that we do is because of what Jesus Christ has done and has accomplished. Everything else, like education and all of our training, are just tools in the hand of the Master to make us better at what God has called us to do. Principal #14) We must bind the strong man. Matthew 12:29, "Or again how can anyone enter a strong man's house and carry off his possessions unless he first ties up the strong man then he can rob the house". When dealing with principalities and powers of darkness, and when dealing with things beyond the human realm, it is important that if we are going to be a success, that we first bind the strong man and then we can go ahead in the name of Jesus, and we can bring healing to the other parts of the personality. So often, in the healing process and in the session work, when a personality gets close to coming to healing, a demon will pop out and at that point, that's when we talk to the demon, get his name, we bind him, and we bind all of his helpers to him, and we command the demons to go. We bind them, gag them, and we command them not to hurt the body, not to manifest, the only choice they have is to go and once you bind the strong man and all the connecting demons, then you are truly able to help that section of the personality come into healing. So many times, during the satanic ritual abuse when multiple personalities are formed, they are told that the demons are good and that the demons are their helpers. So when they are

33

bound, gagged, and when Jesus takes them away, they can see the demons for what they really, and truly are. Principal #15) The ministry of angels and session work. Hebrews 1:14, "Are not all angels ministering spirits sent to serve those who will inherit salvation". One of the things that I have found very helpful in session work and in working with people who are S.R.A. and who have M.P.D., I always pray and ask the Lord to bring in His angels. I always pray and ask Jesus to surround us with his warring and ministering angels. I also pray that when we're in session, and I pray it for the one working with me, that God would send His angels to our homes to protect us while we are doing the work of the ministry. And so often when we have bound and gagged the demons, and chained them together in the name of Jesus, I ask for the angels of God, the angels of heaven to come, and to take the demons away and to bring them to the feet of Jesus and then we ask the Lord to send the demons where he would want them to go. And once again, the important thing to remember, this is not our work, this is not done by our might, human might, or human understanding, this is done by the might of God. When you stand in that authority, one can cast out devils and see a person set free in just a matter of minutes, and yet, when you try to do this with purely human understanding and training, you can't get the work done. The ministry and work of angels is key in understanding the principals of spiritual warfare. While one is working with the angels, we have to be careful that we test also those spirits, to see whether they be from God. Before any session starts or when we're asking for the ministry of angels, we also bind false angels of light that would want to come and deceive and let us think that they are the angels from the heavenly throne. So, it is good to bind the demonic realm and the spiritual forces of darkness that would want to come and portray themselves as agents of light. Principal #16) The power of love. I Corinthians 13:1-8, "If I speak in the tongues of men and of angels but have not love I am only a resounding gong or a clanging symbol. If I have the gift of prophecy and can fathom all mysteries and all knowledge and if I have a faith that can move mountains but have not love, I am nothing. If I give all I possess to the poor and surrender my body to the flames but have not love, I gain nothing. Love is patient, love is kind, love does not envy, love does not boast, it is not proud, it is not rude, it is not self seeking, it is not easily angered, it keeps no records of wrong, love does not delight in evil, but rejoices with the truth. It always protects, it always trusts, it always hope, and it always perseveres. Love never fails but where there are prophecies they shall cease and where there are tongues they will be still and where there is knowledge it will pass away". Probably one of the most important things when dealing with S.R.A.M.P.D. is the power of love. When you are dealing with someone who used to be in the occult, used to worship Satan, has multiple personality disorder and who feels rejected, not only by the world, but by most of the Christian community, it's good that they see that we love them in an unconditional way. That we do not look at them as being weird, but we look at them as a person whom God died for, whom God can set free by the power of His love and the tools that he has given the body of Christ. So one of the very important things for them to see and understand is that they are loved, and we must show them an unconditional love. And, Principal #17) Remember God's promises. I'm not going to quote the scriptures, I'm just going to give the scripture references, these are promises that will help survivors of satanic ritual abuse and who are also multiple personality. These are promises that will help them in their healing and help them to fight against the enemy. The Bible says in Joel 2:25-26 that God would repay us for all the years the locusts have eaten. Also when we come to Christ, we are put in a new bloodline. Often in Satanism, they are told they are from an evil bloodline and that they can never get out of that, but when we come to Christ, II Cor. 5:17-21 tells us that we become a new creature in Christ Jesus and we are put in a new bloodline. Prov. 21:30-31 nothing can succeed against the plans of God. Mark 16:15-20 tells us that, also, laying hands on the sick and seeing them healed, this is the inheritance of the believer. Mark 16:15-20 says healing is in the atonement. Isaiah 53:4-5 tells us that, by His stripes we are healed. Galatians 3:13 tells us that, we have been redeemed from the curse. Proverbs 26:2 tells us, curse without cause cannot light us, in other words, if someone curses us, unless there's an open door or a crack in our armor, that curse can't affect us. Hebrews 4:12-13 tells us, God has given us a sharp two-edged sword in His word. Isaiah 49:25, our captors must show our children mercy. People in Satanism are often told that if they come to Christ, their children will be killed. The scripture says that when you come to the Lord Jesus Christ that those who hold your children captive must show them mercy. The final and wonderful promise that we are given in the word and I will quote this is Revelation 20:10, "And the devil who had deceived them was thrown into the lake burning with sulfur where the beast and the false prophet had been thrown, they will be tormented day and night forever and ever". So the great and marvelous, promise that we have in the word of God is this, that when you read the end of the Bible, you see that we win and Satan loses. That he is a loser and he knows it, he knows that someday he will be cast into the lake of fire.

These seventeen principals that I have mentioned are just some of the basic principals based on the word of God that we have used in session work as it relates to S.R.A.M.P.D. We have used these basic principals over and over and over again. I praise God for the fact that the word of God never gets old and the power in the word of God never fades away. I want to say this in the closing of this chapter; we still have a lot to learn. There has been so much that God has written in His word. As you read the word it's amazing how many new things we see about the word that can help us in our day-to-day battle; we need to stay humble, armed with the full armor of God and we need to stay always in the presence of God and feeding off His word. We must never try to run on our own strength and we must never try to fight in our own power. We must stay in His presence like Moses stayed in the tent of meeting. He spent time with the Lord and then he went out and ministered to the people, but when he was done, he went back into the tent of meeting and he spent time talking to God. And when Jesus spent time with his disciples, they would minister to the people, and then they go up on the mountain and Jesus would spend time with the Father, he would talk with the Father, then He would go out and minister to the people. And one of the things that Jesus said is that He only did what He saw His Father doing.

# CHAPTER THREE

# DIAGNOSING S.R.A.M.P.D.

I believe when diagnosing S.R.A.M.P.D. it's very important to ask two questions, Number 1) what is satanic ritual abuse? And, number 2) what is multiple personality disorder? In this chapter we'll not only discover what is satanic ritual abuse and what is multiple personality disorder, but we'll talk about some of the symptoms and how to go about diagnosing accurately S.R.A.M.P.D.

What is satanic ritual abuse? "Ritual abuse is any systematic pattern or practice practiced by an individual or a group toward children. (Or adults who are emotionally or physically unable to resist or escape) That constitutes abusive power in order to harm and control the victim. Such practices may sometimes appeal to some higher authority or power and justification of the actions taken. This abuse may be mental, physical, emotional, spiritual, or sexual".

"Ritual abuse is aimed at deepening the silence of the already powerless, the poor, the young, the innocent, the used, and the desperate. Victims are often forced to engage in promiscuous and or sadistic acts, sacrifices in which one or more persons are killed, cannibalism, pornography, drug abuse, and other provocative and cruel abuses. Society's denial of the experience of ritual abuse must be recognized as an enabling stance that assists in the continued perpetration of these heinous acts. First of all, ritual abuse is about secrecy, power and total control. Secondly, ritual abuse is torture. It is a calculated effort on the part of perpetrators to systematically brainwash victims through physical, emotional, sexual, and spiritual violation. Thirdly, perpetrators attempt to destroy basic human values and inculcate their own distorted belief system. Through the use of mental coercion and physical torture they are able to gain control of a victim's though process and behavior. Fourthly, there is an attempt to distort a victim's sense of self and reality so that he/she feels personally responsible for the heinous acts of violence, which are being committed. Fifthly, the child/victim is trained to make and enact violent decisions and to believe that the desire to behave that way comes out of their own innate evil. Therefore, victims are often unable to hold their perpetrators responsible. **Sixthly, many cult rituals violate state and/or national laws. Abuse can include promiscuous and/or sadistic sexual acts, sacrifices, cannibalism and other provocative and cruel abuses. Seventh, ritualistic crimes are generally motivated by the perpetrators' desire to control and abuse the victims. Any ideology can be sued as a justification or a framework for abuse. Eighth, often victims are programmed to kill themselves if they ever reveal information about specific rituals and/or the organizational structure and leadership within the cult. Satanic ritual abuse is very different from normal child abuse in that the abusers are not merely acting out their own sickness or unresolved rage from their own childhood abuse. Cult abusers are following prescribed ways of preparing children for cult membership and receptivity to Satan's demands. The following goals of ritual abuse are conscious and distinguish it from more commonly recognized child abuse. There are four basic goals: 1) Specifically promotes certain forms of dissociation which will result in splitting or fragmentation of self-identity. This increases susceptibility to cult control and is believed to foster astral projection (out of body experiences), which is an important ability to develop in the cult. 2) Targets the elimination of all spontaneous emotional feelings or even a unique sense of self. Basically the cult wants to create "robots" to be programmed and directed according to cult rules and purposes. Emotions are only to be elicited at the convenience of the cult in service of certain tasks or learning's. 3) Purposefully**

41

interferes with important early developmental processes such object constancy and promotes a perpetual fear of abandonment. The cult intervenes often with infants and toddlers to destroy basic attachments (switching mother figures), which would normally promote internal security. 4) Ensures the longevity of the cult by utilizing brainwashing techniques resulting in periods of amnesia for cult involvement while guaranteeing cult control. Free will has no place in orthodox Satanism, and the cult does not allow members to leave without significant retaliation".

The second question we want to answer is, what is multiple personality disorder? "Multiple personality disorder MPD is perhaps the most creative, intelligent and elegant coping mechanism and survival technique humans are capable of creating. The foundation of MPD is "dissociation", a psycho-physiological response that enables a person to block especially horrible experiences such as child abuse from his or her memory. According to Frank Putnam, a psychiatrist at the National Institute of Mental Health and a leading expert in the study of multiplicity, MPD has its origin in children before the age of 10-12 usually as the result of the worst kind of physical, sexual, emotional and mental abuse and often in the preverbal child before age 5. At a point when the abuse exceeds the child's ability to accept into his consciousness, some children simply say, "this is not happening". But of course it is happening, so in the beginning of the incredibly complex process the child creates another personality to absorb the pain and terror that threaten to overwhelm the core personality or the birth person. The ability to hand off this pain and torture to an alter personality helps the child survive. As the abuse continues especially in the case of ritualistic or satanic abuse, more personalities may be created to take the torment. In the case of satanic ritual abuse the cult perpetrators may actually induce further fragmenting of the personality system by creating a cult split. This newly created alter personality, often called Satanic, ritual or evil, is generally programmed to adhere to cult ideology without question. Over time the child's alter personalities may become more complete and to some extent autonomous, often having major responsibilities such as performing the core personality's daily work. What began as a survival mechanism often becomes a stumbling block for those with MPD and may even prevent them from leading a healthy, functional life. For instance, at the first sign of even routine stress the alters can take over or switch in an effort to deal with a problem and protect the core personality; however, the core personality never learns to deal with pain, disappointment, fear and other crises of daily life".

So multiple personality disorder happens when through trauma, physical, sexual or mental abuse the personality splits and other alter personalities are formed to handle the pain and the experiences of the memory of the abuse. Many Christians today struggle with the fact that multiplicity exists. Multiplicity is often dismissed as faking or the presence of demons but I believe in God's sovereignty, God has provided a unique way to preserve the love, joy, peace, patience, kindness, goodness, faithfulness, and gentleness in a person's life in the midst of tragedy and extreme abuse. This provision is called multiple personality disorder. A good picture for multiplicity can be found I Corinthians 12:12-28 and I quote, "The body is a unit though it is made up of many parts and though all of its parts are many they form one body so it is with Christ. For we were all baptized by one spirit into one body whether Jews or Greeks, slave or free and we were all given one spirit to drink. Now the body is not made up of one part but many if the foot should say because I am not a hand I do not belong to the body it would not for that reason cease to be a part of the body. And if the ear should say because I am not an eye I do not belong to the body it would not for that reason cease to be a part of the body. If the whole body were an eye where would the sense of hearing be? If the whole body were an ear where would the sense of smell be? But in fact, God has arranged the parts of the body everyone them just as He wanted them to be. If they were all one part where would the body be? As it is there are many parts but one body. The eye cannot say to the hand I don't need you and the head cannot say to the feet I don't need you on the contrary, those parts of the body that seem to be weaker are indispensable and the parts that we think are less honorable we treat with special honor and the parts that are unpresentable are treated with special modesty. While our presentable parts need no special treatment but God has combined the members of the body and has given greater honor to the parts that lack it so that there should be no division in the body but that its parts should have equal concern for each other. If one part suffers every part suffers with it but if one part is honored every part rejoices with it. Now you are the body of Christ each one of you is a part of it and in the church God has appointed first of all apostles, second prophets, third teachers, then workers of miracles, and also those that have gifts of healing, those able to help others, those with gifts of administration, and those speaking with different kinds of tongues". This is a good picture of multiplicity, although the body of Christ is one yet there are many parts, and this scripture says in verse 25 so that there should be no divisions in the body. Now, we saw from studying Psalms 139 when God knit us together in our mother's womb, when He knit us together, He knit us as one. He knit us with no divisions. When God made the human personality He made it whole. He made it complete. He made it, as even though there are many different facets of the personality, He wove it and he knit us together in our mother's womb as one with no division. But, through satanic ritual abuse, through trauma, through sexual abuse, the personality is split and frayed apart so that the different parts that are abused can handle the torture, the trauma and the abuse that they have suffered.

One important thing to remember when diagnosing S.R.A.M.P.D. is that one person doesn't have all of the answers and one person doesn't know it all. It is good to get two or three evaluations of a particular client to know that you have an accurate assessment of the client's personality and what the client needs. Talking with other professionals working in the same field is key because we can be learning from one another and learning new things that others are learning, so that we can better help our own clients to receive the healing that they so desperately need in an accurate and efficient way. As the body of Christ, we must work as a team to bring people into healing. As we work together as a team, we can use other people's gifts, abilities and anointing to help in bringing a person or a particular client into healing. When one particular person seems to run into a roadblock, the client can be referred to other people working in the same field who can bring that particular client further in the healing.

The following are some of the warning signs of satanic ritually abuse and some of the symptoms one might be looking for when trying to make a diagnosis. "Warning Signs: A Parents Guide. Because Satanism has targeted young people so intensely in the last decade, it is important for parents to be alert to signs in their children of demonic involvement. The teen years seem to be a time when children are especially vulnerable to the influences of the devil. The following is a list of important warning signs that parents should be aware of: 1) Extreme mood changes without any known precipitating cause such as explosive rage with foul language. 2) Satanic symbols displayed on books or in notebooks such as 666, Natas, an inverted cross, the pentagram, a goat's head, the sign of the horn (a hand with the first and last fingers extended upward and the remainder folded down). 3) Withdrawing from family life. 4) Heavy metal and black metal music. 5) Listening for hours to this music. 6) A dramatic change in clothing style such as wearing all black with red accents. 7) Abusing drugs. 8) Change in the peer group such as leaving a more normal group to associate with a secretive group. 9) Staying out all night, especially on Friday night, at the time of the full moon, and on Satanist ceremonial days. 10) Falling grades as well as many unexcused absences. 11) Any sign of inhumanity to man or animals, such as cruelty, talking of blood, and a tendency toward macabre scenes. 12) Beginning nightmares and a change in sleep patterns. 13) Noticeable change in facial expression, especially in the eyes in times of rage". These are some good warning signs that your children or that someone might be becoming involved in satanic activity. Some other symptoms of ritual abuse are: 1) personality change, this could be when a child who is normally loving and easygoing all of sudden becomes aggressive or violent and maybe sexually demonstrative or if a child who is confident becomes fearful and is plagued with nightmares and night terrors, that is another good symptom of ritual abuse. 2) Unreasonable fear. Fears can be expressed in many different ways, abnormal fears are being left with the babysitter or maybe emotional regression to a younger age or clinging to mother or fear of going to the bathroom, fear of eating certain things or certain foods, fears of dying, a child can also develop unreasonable fears as it relates to police officers, clergy, doctors, judges or religious objects such as a crucifix or a particular picture of Jesus or even cartoon characters might suddenly become frightening. There could also be the fear of small places or being in a box. A sudden fear of water or being kidnapped or fears of colors such as black or red or purple could be good cause for suspicion. Fears are normal in children or people but patterns of strong fears and anxieties should be thoroughly explored. Another symptom might include sexual symptoms such as the abnormal anxiety of having the genitals washed, or excessive genital play, or a boldness in touching the genitals of other children, or becoming sexually seductive beyond a child's age level. This may also be another good sign of ritual abuse. Another symptom would be emotional changes. Watch for those emotional behaviors that have not been normal in a child's life or in a person's life such as anger, rage, desire to hurt others, or even threatening to kill a family member, this may be also another symptom of ritual abuse, that could go along with mutilate dolls, cutting off the heads, or wanting to use a knife destructively. And also, be very wary of sudden unexplainable mood changes such as temper tantrums and lastly, physical symptoms. Some of the things to watch for would be somatic complaints such as nausea or stomach pain. Or even the fear of swallowing saliva or the fear of having to eat feces or drink urine. The list of symptoms could be much longer but the principle is this, to pay attention to sudden changes in personality, likes and dislikes, fears and anxiety levels or other departures from normal patterns in the child's or adult's life".

"The following are some of the symptoms of multiple personality disorder. 1) Experiencing a loss of time or having amnesia where you cannot remember a certain period of time in their life, for example, I've had people say to me "you know what, my car was moved in a whole different spot and I do not remember driving it", or "all of a sudden I noticed that I was all wet and my clothes were all dirty as if I'd been crawling through the mud and I don't remember doing it". A loss of a block of time where there has been activity but they can't remember is a good symptom. Another symptom is hearing internal voices in the head or hearing voices on the inside. Often people who are schizophrenic will hear voices on the outside but people who are multiple personality will hear voices on the inside. Thirdly, feeling as if someone else had taken over his or her body. Fourthly, strong mood swings accompanied by changes in perceptions, values, behaviors, feelings, attitudes, likes and dislikes. Fifthly, flashbacks that result in memories of abuse or trauma from childhood. Sixthly would be sleep disturbances with night terrors or nightmares. Seventh, could be eating disorders. Eighth, could be addictions to things like alcohol, substances, work, eating, sexual, etc. Ninth, another good indication would be a history of dysfunctional relationships within the family. Tenth, would be self-destructive behaviors such as self-mutilation or suicide attempts. And eleventh would be a history of childhood abuse usually including sexual abuse by caregivers that is severe, prolonged, and reaching the proportions of torture. Some more

49

symptoms of multiple personality disorder; "1) Compulsive re-exposure to the trauma. It has been documented that abused some may be attracted to men who mistreat them and sexually molested children may grow up to become prostitutes. This reenactment of the trauma may result in causing harem to others, being self-destructive or in revictimization. 2) Little or no memories regarding childhood. In many cases multiples will have only selective memories of certain experiences of their childhood. They may remember people and places but few, if any, events. Some multiples remember certain good things, or they may even idealize the past in such a manner that they are unaware of any trauma. 3) Amnesia, the classic understanding of amnesia is no longer a requirement for a definitive diagnosis of DID. It is important to note, however, that some forms of amnesia are usually present but are masked by the internal organization of Alters, who are committed to covering up loss of time. Sometimes amnesia is minimized by the host and explained away as just a poor memory. 4) Trance-like behaviors. Some trance-like behaviors are very obvious, such as frequently staring off into space or being lost in deep thought. Others may be manifested more subtly and can frequently be covered up so that they are not observable by most outsiders. These include frequent loss of the train of thought in conversation, a wandering mind or breaks in concentration while listening. 5) Switches. It is helpful to observe a multiple changing from one Alter to another, but sometimes the switches are imperceptible, even to the multiple. Inconsistencies in perspective, feelings and logic can sometimes provide a clue. Other indicators may be changes in facial expression, habits, handedness, and handwriting. These changes may be observed over minutes, days, weeks, or even longer periods of time. Listen for use of the pronoun we, although often the Alter personalities will avoid its use because it might give them away. 6) Frequent headaches. Not all multiples report frequent headaches, which can be associated with internal conflict between personalities or frequent switching. 7) Medical symptoms with no medical reason. Frequent trips to the doctor or hospitalizations with many different tests and even exploratory surgery may yield no definitive medical explanation for symptoms sometimes experienced by multiples. Professionals in the medical community who have no understanding of the dynamics of the dissociative disorders may label such persons as merely trying to get attention. At other times a trip to the emergency room because of severe pain will cause embarrassment when the pain leaves just before a doctor can be seen. 8) Body memories. These memories occur in the form of physical bruises, scratches or pain in any part of the body that cannot be explained by any current experience. Frequently abdominal pain is reported. The pain may also be centered in the sexual organs but be expressed as a stomachache. When there is not present explanation, it is possible that past traumata is being remembered by the body. The other dissociated parts of the memory may or may not be close enough to the surface to be recovered in therapy at that particular time.

51

Sometimes the full memory will be held by one or more personalities other than the one out at the time the body memory is experienced. 9) Decrease in the ability to function. There are seven points to this inability to function: 1) fluctuating intellectual and creative skills; 2) confusion about time-they may occasionally be confused about what just happened or whether an incident occurred a few hours, days or weeks ago; 3) confusion over possessions; 4) confusion over responsibility for behavior; 5) abnormal fears; 6) flashbacks-some memories will come as dreams or even like a movie being flashed before them in broad daylight. They may remember strange behaviors by friends or loved ones, which they cannot understand; and 7) low self-esteem".

In closing, this chapter is meant to be a tool to help someone in diagnosing someone who may be ritually abused and who may have multiple personalities. This chapter is not a definitive diagnostic tool but rather it is meant to help in the diagnostic process. Once again, I cannot stress enough at the close of this chapter to get a very accurate evaluation of a client. One needs to work as a team with other professionals working in the same field. Also, it is good to get two to three evaluations of one client to make sure of an accurate diagnosis, to make sure that we know what the client really and truly needs. Another reason to get more than one diagnosis is because there are several disorders that can be closely associated with the multiple personality disorder. These disorders are: dissociative disorders, borderline personality disorder, mood disorder, schizophrenia, and post traumatic stress disorder, have been chosen to be examined since they have some symptoms in common that may be confusing to a lay person. That is why it is crucial that two or three evaluations are done on one client so that it can be accurately assessed on how a counselor or psychologist can go about furthering the healing of a client.

There is much to be learned about S.R.A.M.P.D. and that is why we need each other and the body of Christ, we need the help of other professionals in our field, and we need to work as a team as it relates to helping bringing people into healing.

*John Clark PhD*

# CHAPTER FOUR

## A PASTOR'S PERSPECTIVE OF M.P.D. AND THE ROLE OF THE CHURCH FROM A SURVIVOR'S PERSPECTIVE

Having pastored a church for over nine years, I know the reality of the fact that when we're dealing with people who have been satanically ritually abused and who also have multiple personality disorder, that it is very hard for people within the local congregation to accept that. "The things unseen do exist. Both of those areas embrace real facts. But they are such that our ordinary five senses cannot ever discover them. The man who limits himself to what his natural senses can encounter will live all his days sadly impoverished. He will miss the greater reality". And as a pastor, I want to just say for a moment that even churches today struggle with the fact of spiritual warfare. A lot of them want to deny the fact that some of their members have been satanically ritually abused and some of them do have a real disorder called multiple personality disorder. The hard thing for the church to grasp is that this isn't something you can see with your physical eyes, but it is something that you do experience and is something that is real. Faith is a reality, faith is the evidence of things not seen and yet hoped for. So as Christians and pastors, we must be aware if we only deal with the world that is seen, we're only dealing with half of a reality. The other half of the reality is the world that is unseen. I think churches are trying to grow today, and more and more churches today are accepting people who have been satanically ritually abused and are accepting multiple personality disorder as a real spiritual disorder. But the problem still exists in a lot of churches. They deny that it exists or say that multiple personality disorders are demons. And we know neither is true. We know that multiple personality disorder is actually a psychological disorder where the personality is split through trauma and abuse.

As I have worked with people who have been ritually abused and who had multiple personality disorder, one of my privileges was to work with Pastor Jim Casey. When I first met Pastor Jim Casey, he really felt like multiple personality disorder were mainly demons. Then I asked him to write a section for this book from his view point because over his years of ministry, he has helped set the captives free, he has also worked with lots of people who have been ritually abused and who had multiple personality disorder. So Pastor Jim Casey wrote the following article and quote. "Multiple Personality Disorder, A Pastoral Perspective by Pastor Jim Casey. Introduction: Problems in Approaching the Subject. There are several problems in trying to discuss M.P.D. from a pastoral perspective: 1) The psychological community first identified the condition and it's causes. The Christian world until recently hasn't even dealt with the condition. 2) While the psychological community believes the condition to be purely physiological, the church has assumed just the opposite, that the problem is spiritual, i.e. demonic possession. 3) Even those within the community of Christ who do agree that M.P.D. can be a physiological disorder grapple with the proper way to approach treatment. For example, how does a dissociative state impact personal responsibility when a person sins as a personality they are not even aware exists? And 4) There are no scriptural precedents that tell us such a physiological condition exist".

"Diagnosis from a Biblical Perspective. A short review of the biblical teaching concerning original sin and the fall of man will put my comments in their proper context. The scriptures teach that before Adam and Eves' fall from grace they were without sin. To be without sin really means that man's basic integrity; his wholeness and purity in identity with God, are intact. Adam and Eves' worldview contained no conflict, and their hearts were

57

united in their view of things with God. The Lord was their life-giver, physically and spiritually. As triune beings created by God their health, body, soul and spirit, were dependent upon their continued union with the Creator. The results of the fall brought death in every way. The ground was cursed, opening the Pandora's box of deteriorating environment. Man died spiritually; cut off from vital union with God. All subsequent generations were born in sin. What does it mean to be born in sin? It means every propensity in man's heart was toward evil rather than good. This corruption reached its zenith in the days of Noah: Genesis 6:9-12, "This is the account of Noah. Noah was a righteous man, blameless among the people of his time, and he walked with God. Noah had three sons, Shem, Ham and Japheth. Now the earth was corrupt in God's sight and was full of violence. God saw how corrupt the earth had become, for all the people on earth had corrupted their ways". The Hebrew word used for corrupt and corrupted in this passage is shahat, which is translated in English as both destroy and corrupt. The idea is that mankind as a whole was ruined. That is the idea presented throughout scripture; mankind was ruined by the fall. When we talk about whether or not M.P.D. is a real disorder, a more fitting question from the Christian perspective would be this: Given the condition of man after the fall, could M.P.D. be one of the possible results of the devastation of sin? The answer, with some biblical explanation, is yes. Some people with M.P.D., seem to be aware of their other personalities to some degree, others claim no awareness whatsoever. In both cases they are not integrated personalities. The key issue has to do with if someone can do something and not be aware of it, or at least of the reasons/motives behind it. The psychological community calls this state of mind disassociation: Disassociation is a disturbance in the normally integrative functions of memory and consciousness. Thoughts or behaviors are to some degree-disconnected from the mainstream of a person's identity. The disturbance may range from mild to sever and from chronic to sudden. The extreme is observed in multiple personality disorder. Dissociation is also manifested in symptoms of psychosis such as delusions, in symptoms of hysterical neurosis, in sleepwalking, in some forms of amnesia, and in automatic writing. Many phenomena of hypnosis are the result of temporary dissociation. (Academic American Encyclopedia Vol. 6, pg. 198) Does the scripture support that view? Let's look at a few: Romans 7:14-25, "We know that the law is spiritual; but I am unspiritual, sold as a slave to sin. I do not understand what I do. For what I want to do I do not do, but what I hate I do. And if I do what I do not want to do, I agree that the law is good. As it is, it is no longer I myself who do it, but it is sin living in me. I know that nothing good lives in me, that is, in my sinful nature. For I have the desire to do what is good, but I cannot carry it out. For what I do is not the good I want to do; no, the evil I do not want to do, this I keep on doing. Now if I do what I do not want to do, it is no longer I who do it, but it is sin living in me that does it. So I find this law at work:

59

when I want to do good, evil is right there with me. For in my inner being I delight in God's law; but I see another law at work in the members of my body, waging war against the law of my mind and making me a prisoner of the law of sin at work within my members. What a wretched man I am! Who will rescue me from this body of death? Thanks be to God, through Jesus Christ our Lord! So then, I myself in my mind am a slave to God's law, but in the sinful nature a slave to the law of sin".

"Paul the apostle makes clear we can be doing things we know are wrong and not understand why. So then, we can certainly be in a disassociative state (unaware of) concerning our motivations for what we do. Paul attributes this to being a slave to the sinful nature. And as astonishing as it may appear, we are never told that the answer to this problem is to understand ourselves. The remedy for this condition is discussed later in this book under treatment. Another scripture supporting this idea is found in the book of Proverbs 20:5, "The purposes of a man's heart are deep waters, but a man of understanding draws them out". If a man's motivations are so hidden from him that it requires a counselor to help him gain proper perspective, then we can rightly conclude this to be a disassociative state. Again in the scripture we read, Jeremiah 17:9, "The heart is deceitful above all things and beyond cure. Who can understand it?"

"This theme concerning the heart's deceitfulness and inability to be cured is a major them throughout scripture and the very reason our Lord had to come save us! We've established that a man's motivation can be hidden from him. The next questions to ask is: Can a separate personality from our own be within us and yet completely hidden from us? The answer to this from a scriptural perspective is purely speculative, for the scripture talks strictly in terms of demonic personalities being present, and then there is never an instance cited where we can say with certainty the person possessed is unaware of the possession. While not able to speak with certainty scripturally, I will offer my opinion based on personal experience".

"In one instance, I received a call from a family in our church whose teenage son was suffering from violent fits of rage. When I say violent I am not exaggerating, for the boy would become both homicidal and suicidal. We had a number of counseling sessions together and thoroughly examined scripture concerning anger and the right way to deal with it. There was no discernable positive difference as a result of our counseling together. One night, his mother called me asking me to come to their house because he was having on of his fits. As I drove to their home I cried out to God as to why this was happening and what I could do. I was made to know by the Holy Spirit that two demonic spirits were afflicting the boy, one tempting him to suicide and the other to despair. I was shocked at this and asked the Lord how a Christian could be possessed by a demon (the strong impression I received was the young man was possessed). No reply from God was forthcoming by the time I reached the house. As I came into the living room I saw the boy seated in a chair, his head turned to the side and tears steaming down his face.  In an effort to gain some time while I waited to see if God would give me more direction I asked the family to tell me all about what had happened.  Finally, I again felt the Holy Spirit speak to my heart: "Why don't you just bind the demons?" a suggestion that greatly relieved me because I did not want to address them as they were possessing the boy for fear of what the family might think.  I stood before the boy and said "In the name of Jesus Christ you vile spirits of suicide and despair".  Before I could get another word out the young man threw his head up and screamed at the top of his voice.  Then his whole body pitched forward up and out of the chair and he landed face first, with his hands down at his sides, on the hardwood floor.  When I saw him two days later, his face was black and blue all along one side.  Obviously there were demons there and they were within the young man.  Now, I don't believe a Christian can be demon possessed, and this young man thought he was a Christian; but the facts are the facts.  I led him through the sinners' prayer and prayed for him to be filled with the Holy Spirit, which the Lord graciously did do.  Since that time he has not had a reoccurrence of that condition.  My point in bringing up the story is that here is a case where someone did not know a separate personality from his own inhabited his physical body".

"In another instance a teenage boy was visiting our church along with his mother and two brothers.  At the end of the service the mother requested prayer for a number of needs.  We usually do an inventory of the persons past before praying. We discovered she had been heavily involved with the occult in her life at some time, so we asked the Lord to remove any demonic influences from her life and the lives of her children. Immediately she fell down as demonic spirits came out of her, and her oldest son went into full-blown demonic possession. This was by far the worst case of possession I had ever witnessed, for the demons with the boy growled at us in perfect imitation of a lion. As they did every muscle in the boy's body enlarged so much that he went from looking like a normal man to a huge body builder in a matter of seconds. Then the possessed boy came at us as if to harm us. Four of us prayed with that boy for an hour and a half before he was set free. During that time, he came out of possession for brief periods scared to death because he was not aware there were demon personalities within him. In each case, the people involved testified they were not aware of the possession. So, my opinion is that people can certainly have a demonic personality possessing them they are unaware of. Now we come to the question of whether a persona can have a multiple personality disorder apart from demonic involvement. I am indebted to Pastor Richard Goldsmith, a Nationally Certified Counselor for the genesis of my following argument. When discussing this issue with him one day, his question to me was; "Dave, why doesn't anyone talk about the Multiple Personality Order as seen in the Godhead?" He went on to say that, having been created in God's image; we reflect something of that multiple personality order. How? Well, in that we all have multiple roles we fulfill in this life. As with God, the majority of us will be fathers and sons (mothers and daughters) at one time or another. God is described as both, and we reflect His image. Now, if we are able to fulfill different roles and stay a unified personality, doesn't our faith, logic, and experience suggest that the opposite may be true? Can't we assume that, as a result of sins destruction in a person's life, they may become disunited in personality, even to the point of acting out subconsciously other lives? Is it possible? I believe we have the scriptural framework to make that conclusion".

"We Christians are in danger of acting like know-it-alls concerning what the possible outcome of the shattering effect of sin might be in someone's life. To demonstrate, let me use the illustration of a broken glass. Before breaking, anyone can by observation tell a lot about how a glass should be and in fact is constructed. Trying to predict exactly how it will shatter when dropped, however, is a fool's game. Even should twenty identical glasses be dropped in the same exact way, not one will shatter in exactly the same manner. And how much more varied are the people and circumstances in this life than those manufactured glasses! Therefore, it is safe to conclude the scriptures concede the possibility of a person acting out different personalities while not even being aware they are doing so".

"Treatment. My concern as a pastor for those who need help is that they find competent caregivers for this highly unusual situation. I would not refer people from my church unless there is competency demonstrated in the following".

"Providing a proper foundation and framework from the scriptures. I Corinthians 4:6, "Now I have applied all this about parties and factions to myself and Apollos for your sakes, brethren, so that from what I have said of us as illustrations you may learn to think of men in accordance with scripture and not to go beyond that which is written, that none of you may be puffed up and inflated with pride and boast. (The Amplified Bible)"

"Over the years, as I've interacted with people from different counseling and deliverance ministries, I have been deeply disturbed by the tendencies of some counseling ministries to abandon the framework of scripture because of the success of technique they have supposedly been shown by divine revelation. I do not find fault with their motives; these are deeply compassionate people who have explored waters the majority of us would not dare to traverse. However, I have found this to be a fundamental truth we must not abandon: We must always operate upon the foundation and within the framework of the written revelation of God's word. Some claim to have received revelation from God that has not a shred of biblical foundation, and then proceed to claim written revelation unnecessary. For some, the inability to discern anything scriptural that would apply to the present need of their client has caused them to rely on only that which they receive from supernatural revelation. While I understand their frustration, I firmly hold to a second

65

principle every Christian must consider. Not even for the sake of human need are we to abandon the foundation and framework of scripture. To insist we must proceed apart form any direction and often in contradiction given in scripture is to have already given way to deception of believing God doesn't care if we do so. In fact, however, the scripture does provide what we need in every situation. II Timothy 3:16-17, "All scripture is God-breathed and is useful for teaching, rebuking, correcting and training in righteousness, so that the man of God may be thoroughly equipped for every good work". (NIV) In some deliverance ministries people interrogate demonic spirits that are possessing people in order to get information to set the person free, a practice forbidden in scripture. Leviticus 19:31 "Do not turn to mediums or seek out spiritists, for you will be defiled by them. I am the Lord your God". (NIV) By using a possessed person as an unwitting medium, are we not in violation of God's commands? Not only will we be defiled, but also there is the possibility of other consequences. Leviticus 20:6, "I will set my face against the person who turns to mediums and spiritists to prostitute himself by following them, and I will cut him off from his people". (NIV)

"The Lord himself could very well become angry with us for what amounts to idolatry. Also, those who do so are often isolated from the vast majority of the body of Christ. If we need to wait upon God until He sees fit to provide revelation rooted in the word of God, so be it. Isaiah 8:17-9:2, "I will wait for the Lord, who is hiding his face from the house of Jacob. I will put my trust in him. Here am I, and the children the Lord has given me. We are signs and symbols in Israel from the Lord Almighty, who dwells on Mount Zion. When men tell you to consult mediums and spiritists, who whisper and mutter, should not a people inquire of their God? Why consult the dead on behalf of the living? To the law and to the testimony! If they do not speak according to this word, they have no light of dawn. Distressed and hungry, they will roam through the land; when they are famished, they will become enraged and, looking upward, will curse their king and their God. Then they will look toward the earth and see only distress and darkness and fearful gloom, and they will be thrust into utter darkness. Chapter 9:1-2, "nevertheless, there will be nor more gloom for those who were in distress. In the past he humbled the land of Zebulun and the land of Naphtali, but in the future he will honor Galilee of the Gentiles, by the way of the sea, along the Jordan. The people walking in darkness have seen a great light; on those living in the land of the shadow of death a light has dawned". (NIV) No matter how deep the need is, it is never beyond the reach of God's written word. II Timothy 3:16-17, "All scripture is God breathed and is useful for teaching, rebuking, correcting, and training in righteousness, so that the man of God may be thoroughly equipped for every good work". (NIV) Another practice I find questionable is that of trying to merge separate personalities into one unified whole, with the original dominant birth personality taking charge. All these personalities do not need to merge, they need to die! The Lord never promises to integrate man's personality (ies), but to make us a new creation. II Corinthians 5:14-19, "For Christ's love compels us, because we are convinced that one died for all, and therefore all died. And he died for all that those who live should no longer live for themselves but for him who dies for them and was raised again. So from now on we regard no one from a worldly point of view. Though we once regarded Christ in this way, we do so no longer. Therefore, if anyone is in Christ, he is a new creation; the old has gone, the new has come! All this is from God, who reconciled us to himself through Christ and gave us the ministry of reconciliation: that God was reconciling the world to himself in Christ, not counting men's sins against them. And he has committed to us the message of reconciliation". (NIV) Galatians 6:14-15, "May I never boast except in the cross of our Lord Jesus Christ, through which the world has been crucified to me, and I to the world. Neither circumcision nor uncircumcision means anything; what counts is a new creation". (NIV)

"Do we trust God enough to take Him at His word? It tells us we are a new creation. Faith comes by hearing, and hearing by the word of God. If we want to see people act like a new creation, we must thoroughly instruct them in the word concerning that truth. Granted, to minister to someone with M.P.D. makes that process difficult, be we have God's promise that if we will ask, knock and seek (a figure of repeatedly inquiring) He will give us the needed wisdom, power and discernment to bring people to full health; body, soul, spirit, thought, will and emotion. In conclusion, let me state I am a seeker of truth still, and if anyone reading these words can offer scriptural insights that will cause me to amend some of the things sated in this treatise, please contact me. After all, our goal in this life is not to be right, but to be true. True to Him who is the Way, Truth, and Life".

I included Pastor Jim Casey's thoughts in this book because I wanted the reader to understand and know the real struggle that there is in the hearts of our pastors in understanding this disorder. Do I fully agree with everything that he has written? For the most part, I fully agree with everything Pastor Jim Casey has written. He is a good friend and a good colleague grounded in the word of God, and he is definitely a seeker of truth. He told me that after writing for this book that he now believes that multiple personality disorder is a true disorder, but there is still a lot that needs to be learned about this disorder and he still has a lot of questions about the subject. But in the case of asking the demon a question, I do not believe it is wrong because even Jesus himself asked the man running through the tombs who violently cut himself, He asked that demon what his name was and the demon said, "our name is Legion, for we are many", and at that point Jesus commanded Legion and all the demons to go into the herd of swine who ran into the lake and were drowned. So we do see that there is biblical precedent for getting a demons name. But I think that is not necessarily always the norm. We should not, and this is where I agree with Pastor Casey also, we should not be

69

interrogating demons and asking them all questions because they are just liars and they serve the father of lies. Another point that Pastor Casey makes is about the integration of the personality. I do agree that we all must learn to die to ourselves and be crucified with Christ but what I think we also need to understand is that only Jesus knows how to put the personality back together. After one has died to self, it's really up to Jesus and the power of the Holy Spirit to do the integration process. The scripture says that God knit us together in our mother's womb and only God truly knows how to put us back together. No amount of psychological education or human understanding can do that, we must depend on the revelation, on the Holy Spirit, on the word of God and the power of God to get the process done.

Now as it relates to the role of the church in dealing with people who are surviving from satanic ritual abuse and multiple personality disorder, I just want to say that this is like virgin territory. This is frontier territory because 99.9% of the churches today have not learned to deal with people that have come out of the occult, people who have been ritually abused, and people who have multiple personality disorders. These people have been treated as though they have been demonized and are normally outcast and pushed away from the church. But praise God there are a number of churches raising up in the face of the earth, who are starting and beginning to learn how to deal with survivors from ritual abuse who have multiple personalities. In the book Journey to Wholeness, "Those of us involved in the healing community need to be willing to do four things: 1) We must be willing to take an interest in the people God brings our way. The people God brings into our church are not perfect; they are incomplete, and may be fragmented. Sometimes, they can be rather obnoxious and difficult. Yet, we need to learn to see them as God sees them, not just as they appear. They all have the potential to become all God created them to be. God expects us to reach out to them and minister healing, no matter how difficult the situation may seem. 2) We need to be willing and prepared to make intercession for people through communication with them, and through prayer on their behalf. I know of a church that formed a group of couples called Shepherds. These couples had four or five new Christians assigned to them whom they took a genuine interest in, and minister to. Of course, the shepherds pray for them, interceding on their behalf. Would it not be wonderful to know that there was someone who is praying for you specifically? How reassuring it would be to know that someone was watching over you in love, to be there for nurturing, guidance, and during times of crisis. It is difficult to minister to people when you have no idea what their needs really are. 3) We need to be willing to make intervention, that is, to intervene when there are problems in people's lives. I do not mean an intrusionary intervention, saying or doing things against an individual's will; rather, being willing to listen and care, willing to give assistance and nurturing, willing to give counsel and prayer, or to find trained resources to assist them if necessary. This may include pastoral care and counseling, or even professional assistance. 4) We need to be involved in the ministry of reconciliation. II Corinthians 5:17 says, "Wherefore, if any man is in Christ he is a new creature, the old things past away behold new things have come. Now all these things are from God who reconciled us from self to Christ and gave us the ministry of reconciliation". The Apostle Paul states here that God has given us the ministry of reconciliation, just as Jesus reconciled us. That ministry is not just to the unsaved, but to the saved as well. We need to be willing to reach out and assist in reconciling people back into a right relationship with God and each other".

In the book Care-Giving The Cornerstone of Healing, Cheryl Knight and Jo Getzinger talk about five things that people in the church can do to help. "1) Determine who can provide friendship support among selected lay persons in the church. These supports need to be able to model healthy relationships and weather a great deal of testing over a long period of time from untrusting personalities. 2) During the healing process, dissociative persons are often plagued with flashbacks and the reliving of repressed memories of the abuse. If there are members of the church who are able to hear some of the memories, the dissociative person will have an important resource for support when unable to reach professional support. 3) Determine what financial support might be needed. The healing process is intensive and often financially draining. Many cannot hold jobs during the healing process due to an inconsistent ability to access skills often because of personality switches and trying to manage difficult memories.  4) Determine the specific needs and the support assistance to be given to the survivor.  5) It has been the authors' experience that multiples with satanic ritual abuse histories have benefited greatly from deliverance work.  This could be offered to them, never forced upon them, when they are ready.  We also recommend that deliverance work be done while the multiple is in therapy.  Even though deliverance work has been done, there will continue to be demonic strongholds until each personality and their memories are healed and resolved".

There is still much to be learned as it relates to the role of the church and there would be great benefit for those working with survivors to contact other churches and other ministries that have a had history of success in working with survivors, to talk with them about what they have learned, what they could be doing, and maybe even what they shouldn't be doing.  The Christian community needs to see itself as a whole, not as fragmented pieces or parts.  It must be a team effort to work with people who are survivors of ritual abuse and have multiple personality disorder.

A survivor who The Lords Messenger and I were working with for over 400 hours wrote the following article.  This particular survivor was living on his property and she wrote an article on the family.  For name's sake, we're going to call her Julie for the protection of her identity.  She wrote on the topic of the family and how she was feeling at the time, going through the healing process.  So as you read the following statement, please take into consideration that the trauma she was going through, and the hurt she was experiencing on the inside. Working with her for over 400 hours in one year, we saw a great need. Also, there needs to be more than two people working with one survivor. It needs to be the body of Christ, and survivors very often long to have a family and that's the very thing they are told in the occult that they'll never have; that a family will never accept them; that the church will always look at them as outcasts. The following is the article on the family that Julie wrote, "Being an SRA dealing with multiple personalities, we on the inside often see and hear things differently than the rest of the world. We get to spend time with Jesus inside, away from pressures of the external forces that rule earth. But we want to encourage every believer to seek that place in the spirit; much like the place we retreat to inside, alone with the Lord. God is no respecter of persons, and He can teach his children how to live in the spirit and find the same kind of closeness we often enjoy. Soon, we will be whole. We began as one and will return to that state of one heart, one mind and one personality. But before we enjoy that healing, Jesus wanted us to share something with the rest of believers. Many will get offended by what we are about to say. Others will discard it because we are not married and have no family. But truth is truth, whether the one delivering it has the same life experiences of the hearers or not. Many Christians want to see the church return to the form demonstrated by the first church in the book of Acts. This is a worthy desire, but one

74

which will not be fulfilled unless families return to their calling. Just as the church is to be representative of God's kingdom, so the family is to be representative of the church. Here is where many have failed. There are many forces coming against the family today. Satan is trying to destroy the very foundation of the family. This has had profound impact on this institution in many ways. But the area that has become the most damaged has been that families fear doing the work of the gospel. Christian families have failed to remember that they cannot be "home centric" anymore than God would desire his people to become "ego-centric". God often brings men and women together in marriage to fulfill a calling in ministry that they cannot accomplish separately. He likewise gives children to believers not just for their own pleasure, but because he has a plan and calling on those young lives. He has always needed people to work His plan. That has not changed. But what has changed is that families now believe that the needs of the family must supersede the needs of the gospel. This is not so! The gospel cost God his Son! It is supreme to all other calls. That is not to say that the needs of family aren't important, they are. It is God's will that parents see the needs of their children. But the truth is, Christian families have overdone it. Let us give you an example. If you were out with your family having dinner and as you left the restaurant, you passed a bum lying in the gutter, what would you do? Would you show your children the Pharisee or the Good Samaritan? Many believers would say that it would endanger their kids or family to lend assistance to such a one. Poppy cock! Either God is big enough to protect you or He isn't. Protection is one of the main issues that has led to the lack of families having the big picture of God's plan in the earth before their eyes. We can certainly exercise wisdom. But protection is from God. Proverbs says that the horse is prepared for battle, but victory is from the Lord. It is our command to be wise, but not our job to protect ourselves. That's God's business! The Master is commanded in scripture to protect the servant. We are God's servants. The family today is a lot like we multiples. Each of us was made to protect from hurt. Those of us who have realized that we belong to Jesus and are of the bloodline of Jesus Christ, receive healing and can be whole and do the work of the gospel. It may not be easy to stand up to the dark ones inside who don't believe the gospel. It is difficult to argue with those inside who thing they have to protect. They are the ones who tear down the work the most. They are the ones who keep us from entering into the life God has for us. But as they come to understand the bigger picture of who we are, who God made us to be, and the plan He has for us, the more they get on board with that plan and the more healing and unity we see. And we get stronger, not weaker! Families are like that. There have been families torn apart by ministering to the lost and bound. But the reason they were torn apart was not because the command of the Lord to win the lost and set captives free was only for those who felt their family could take the press of it. It was given to every believer even the smallest believing child! But when the family ceases to instill in each member the fact that each person in the family is a child of God first, and of their parents second, then you cannot raise children who will be able to do the work of the gospel. They will see their needs and their will as supreme to the needs and will of God. They will become exclusive and selfish and be like the dark ones we have inside. They will tear apart the work and the family. This is why we have so few functioning, non-complaining, truly giving member of the body of Christ. Most church going Christians treat the church like their family, their needs come first. But God's word says to prefer one another. And if his word says to do it, then there is a grace to carry it out and He will protect you through it".

"The first church had all things in common and they saw people saved every day! People sold their houses and gave the money to the church. So where did these believers live when they sold their house? They lived with other believers! Sure, it probably brought some resistance from some family members to have their home become so communal. But their mindset was that they had all things in common. You know, deacons of the first church had families too! But they helped those who had no heads of household. How do you think their kids felt about it? Some probably hated it. But those who had been trained to understand the big picture that the most important thing in the world was to see God's will be done and they were key in that will, survived it. They became the next missionaries who carried the gospel. They didn't sit home and say they couldn't reach the lost cause it took too much from their family time. They made the work of the gospel their family time!"

"Alas, we have dug in and huddled, not realizing that each family has a place in the work of the gospel. If you look in the Old Testament, you see that the Levites were the families who were to become priests. Children raised in those families knew that they were called by virtue of their family, to be priests in service to the Lord and the nation. Younger children understood that if their father was away in the temple, it was to do God's work, and God's work always came first. If their big brothers were gone, it was the same. They did not grumble because their parent was doing God's work. They understood the providence of their family and their place in it. One day, with joyful expectation, they would dream that they too would do such work under the hand and anointing of the most Awesome, Powerful God of the universe. They saw it as a privilege, not a detraction from who they were. They were proud of their fathers. They were in awe of the Lord's call and plan for their lives and their family. They saw such a calling as supreme to all others. But today, we see families exalt their needs above the call of God, especially in the North".

"We were appalled when we moved here years ago. We still cannot get used to churches that have cancelled their evening services because of school sporting events. What atrocity! Many say they closed their night services to make more family time. But what better family time is there than to worship the Lord together?  The message this gives the children is that God comes after family.  Wrong!  If God comes before family, the family will stand.  If the plan and will of God is exalted in family life as being the ideal, then the family will prosper".

"If you look in the Old Testament, you see the laws governing family.  Many were established to help those who lost their own families.  Children in the Old Testament knew that their family could be expanded at any time.  If the brother of the father died, the widow and children were brought into the family.  Children understood this.  They didn't see if as hurting their family or jeopardizing their position with their parents.  It expanded their family!  Likewise, orphans and the poor were brought into families.  These kids knew that all Jews were their brothers and sisters.  They grew up with the understanding that they would be taken care of because they saw how God took care of His people.  Every Jewish child was raised with the understanding that they were of their biological parent's house, but they belonged to God, were a part of a tribe and a nation.  They had expanded vision that went beyond their own wants.  They were raised with God consciousness.  This is good.  A child understanding that they are loved by their parents is important.  But only when they know that foremost, they are loved by God, belong to God, and have a divine calling from God, will they ever have purpose and true identity.  Without this knowledge, they will not see ministry as a joyful divine calling, but as a threat.  This is where families fail".

"We need to remember the people of old. Abraham had to lay Isaac on the altar. This was a test of faith, yes, but it also did a work in Abraham's heart. He could not have become the father of many nations if he had not laid his own family on the altar and given them to God. He could not have later taken in Lot and all the others families who came under his covering. Did this destroy his family? No. Isaac became partaker in the promise. He worshipped the Lord, and God gave him many lands. In Genesis 26, God told him He would perform the oath He'd made to Abraham and give Isaac abundance. He, like others of old, knew that the blessing of his father's faith and service to God would come upon him as well".

"Jacob lost part of the vision of the eternal with his sons. We do not read of him seeking God for the blessings and fulfillment of the promise made to Abraham. We see him favoring Joseph and Benjamin because of his love for their mother. We see him rebuking the gift in Joseph when he had the dream of his brothers and mother and father bowing before him. If he had kept the eternal mindset, he would have instilled the vision and exalted the will of God in their hearts. His other sons would have known they had divine purpose and humility would have reigned in the home. But instead, the Lord had to allow Joseph to be sold, taken from his father's house, in order to see his gift and calling fulfilled. God was certainly big enough to have exalted Joseph while he still lived with his father. We see how the Pharaoh sent through all the land looking for someone who could interpret his dreams. Joseph could have come to the forefront then. But God saw that his father had no vision. He saw that Jacob was ruled by his own desires and had become family-centric. It's highly unlikely that Jacob would have let Joseph go and walk in the plan God had for his life. So instead, the Lord allowed him to be sold to set him in a place where he alone could speak to him and build the eternal vision and gift the Lord had for his life. It wasn't until the Lord had exalted Joseph, displayed his divine plan through him, and moving Jacob to Egypt, that we see Jacob obtain that eternal vision. As he lay on his deathbed, he regains his spiritual sight of the blessing of Abraham and the promises of God to his generations".

"Many families of believers now have one or both parents whose families were torn apart by divorce or dysfunction. Because of this, they have grown family-centric. They have fallen into the trap of trying to protect their family at the cost of obeying the gospel. They see helping others as a threat, and anyone with a need as taking away from their family. This is not God's thinking! It's man's self-protective thinking! Every needy person the Lord brings across the path of a family is an opportunity for the family to be expanded and to be blessed. It's an opportunity for the children to see their divine calling as believers. It is opportunity for parents to display God's character to their kids. It's a chance to weed the selfishness from their children by training them to see through God's eyes. And it's the best way the Lord has for healing those wounded parents, by having them help heal others".

"There's another part of this too. Without this training, without this teaching children to understand the calling of the family, you will never teach them right sharing and perspective. No one owns anything in this earth. We all die paupers. We may have cars or houses in our name, but we only steward those thing until we die. We certainly don't take them with us. We need to understand that everything we touch on this earth will pass away. It is only ours to handle temporarily. This is true of children. They are a heritage from the Lord. You do not own a heritage, you leave a heritage. Children are loaned to their parents, but how many parents teach this to their kids? How many teach their kids that they belong to God first, and that his will is supreme? That the work of the gospel is more important than movies or dinners or vacations? What if families took missions trips for a vacation? What if they spent the night as a family working in a soup kitchen instead of dining in a fine restaurant? What if parents encouraged their kids to find friends at school who had no father or mother and ask them to visit and share their parents with those children who had none? Would we begin to see a church arise like the first church? Yes! We would begin to see children who understand that if they and their parents and their family do the work and will of God, they will be taken car of. As they grasp the high calling God has for their family, they will be built up, not torn down. They will see the provision of the Lord for their needs like never before. They will become God dependent, and not people dependent. They will live the words of "Give and it shall be given to you". They will begin seeing God use them as a child and watch Him build the gifts he's placed in them. This is so important. Most believers struggle with trying to be a child of God, while being an adult. Many don't understand childlike faith. This is because they were kept from exercising faith when they were children. They are trained that until they are adults, they cannot be used of God. Just in the past 50 years, we've seen valuable unity stripped from the family. One way this has been done is that families no longer talk about being a unit of use for God. They no longer talk about working together. Children have no chores. They aren't taught that they are a functional, valued member of a team. They are taught instead that their needs are the heartbeat of the family, and not that the family's heart should beat to meet the needs of God's will and plan. Too many have become like the multiple, with all the parts doing their jobs and having their eyes either on self, or protecting and not on the big picture and embracing the truth of who we all are in God and how we are all part of each other. Families need to voice their calling. Parents need to share their gifs and their vision for ministry with their children. They need to let their kids know that they were born into that family to be a part of what God is doing through that family for His glory and to be trained for the day God will use them in their own ministry and call. Some of the most powerful people of God have told of how they were raised. Most had one or both parents who were reinforcing a divine calling on the child's life. I've heard stories of how most were taught at young ages that when they were hurt or had a problem as a child, they should pray for themselves. Their parents would hold them and silently agree with them as they asked God for their needs. And many of the great men of God were used powerfully at young ages because they learned to seek God first as their Father, and their parents second. Some recounted how they were trained that seeking their needs from others was like getting hand me downs, because the availability and who they were in God was so poured into them that they couldn't wait to pray. He became their hero. He became their source. Their parents taught them that they were set to oversee the lives of their children and to introduce them to their true Father and source. Instead of wanting their children to depend on them, these parents instilled within their kids to need to depend on God. They downplayed themselves, and exalted the Lord, keeping the eyes of their little ones on Him and His availability to their kids, and not so much on themselves. They certainly didn't ignore or neglect them. They loved them, cuddled them, spent time with them, and bound up their wounds. They praised them and corrected them. But they never allowed their children to see them as God. They fostered dependence upon the Lord, and not on the parent".

"So how do you see the church become like it was in the Book of Acts? Start with the family. Grab the eternal holy vision.

84

Train children to see their divine purpose and how to minister to one another in the family, and you will begin to raise a generation that will be able to have all things in common. Exalt the needs of the gospel over the wants of the family. Instill unity in the members. Cease trying to do God's job of protecting your home from the lost and hurting that Jesus died for. Embrace the work of the gospel with your kids, and you will see your kids become workers of the gospel. Get out of family-centric thinking and into gospel centered thinking and you'll see the scriptures fulfilled. When Jesus said, "Seek ye first the kingdom of God", he was speaking to his disciples. Decide to be disciples, disciplined in word and deed, individually and together as a family. Remember that many of the disciples had families, and still did the work of the gospel. Jesus commanded all of them to do the ministry, not just the single ones. But he promised that if they sought His kingdom first, everything else would be added to them. Scripture is true. Don't blame ministering to the lost and bound for problems in the family. But realize that once you begin to minister, any problems in the family will surface, like dross, they have to be dealt with and eternal vision has to be applied to them. If your family has been used to focusing on themselves, then begin the process of expanding the family and vision. Begin to praise your children for their accomplishments and add "And you know Honey, I know God is proud of you too and He can use your gifts to help Him reach the world!" See what kind of results you get. When you hear squabbles between siblings, ask them if they think

85

that their behavior is something that can be used for the calling on their life and God's plan for the family. Help them see beyond their wants and grasp their identity as divinely appointed people belonging to the most Awesome God of all! Find out who their heroes are. If your son says he would think it the greatest thing in the world to have Superman ask him to do something for him, then tell him how much better God is than Superman! Teat the calling of God to fulfill the gospel as the greatest honor on earth, because it is! Include them in that call. Let them know that nothing, nothing, absolutely nothing they or you could ever do is greater than working for God. And when the family has time to do something together, why not pray as one and ask God what you should do. If he says to go to the beach, then hallelujah! But ask Him if you should invite the old widow down the street to go with you! Maybe He'd rather have you go visit the elderly in the nursing homes, or go take the snotty nosed kid next door to a ballgame with you. Expand your family and your vision to include all the souls Jesus died for. God's big enough to make it fun for the kids! Just give Him a chance. Teach your own family to have all things in common, for the common goal of seeing the gospel-fulfilled and the Lord's will done on earth through and for the family of Christ. Then, and only then, can we begin to see the church filled with the sharing, eternally minded believers who will see the revival, miracles, and unity of the First Church".

There is much to be explored in the role of the church. We see the different viewpoints, the different viewpoints on what a pastor's perspective is on M.P.D. and we see the S.R.A.'s perspective on the family, the role of the church, and working with the lost, hurting and wounded. There is truly much to be learned and much understanding to be brought into this field as it relates to the role of the church. It takes more than two people to be a family to an S.R.A. It takes the body of Christ. This is where a need for a call for balance, and wisdom comes in. There needs to be teams of people working with the hurting and the wounded so that it all doesn't fall on the shoulders of one person or one family. Churches must work together, people working in this field must band together and share their ideas, they must share what they're learning, they must share what the pitfalls are when dealing with people coming out of Satanism who have multiple personalities, who are highly wounded and can sometimes be highly manipulative and codependent on other people. So it takes wisdom. We must consult professionals, we must talk with people across the country that are having success in this field. The basic role of the church is to be like Jesus and operate as the first church did in the Book of Acts. Also the first church used wisdom, they had structure, and they followed the rules and the regulations that the Apostle set forth in the word of God, we must stick closely to the word. We must treat these people coming out of Satanism who have multiple personalities, with love, with respect, and we must care for them because they are God's wounded warriors, He wants to heal them up for use in His end time battle. The church must be trained, educated, and

87

taught about their position in Christ and that they have nothing to fear by taking these people in.  The church needs to be educated and brought into a new maturity and a new level of growth to handle the influx of these people that will be coming out of the cult, because more and more people are wanting out of Satanism and when they come out, they come out with only the shirt on their back.  So churches need to use wisdom, they need to find out how other people are doing it in other churches.  The role of the churches is basically still being developed because this is a cutting edge ministry and I would say that less that 1% of the body of Christ right now, is willing to deal with it.

# CHAPTER FIVE

# TWO SURVIVORS' PERSPECTIVE ON THE HEALING PROCESS

I can't think of any better way to help survivors of satanic ritual abuse who have multiple personalities come into healing than to hear what they have to say about the process. So often we jump to conclusions and we think we know it all, we think we know how to fix it, and we think we understand exactly what they've gone through when we don't. So I've included in this chapter the words of two survivors that will help us get a view of what it is like to go through the healing process.

Jackie is a survivor of satanic ritual abuse, she was a multiple, and this is what she has to say about healing. "Will it ever go away? Will it ever go away? Those feelings I experience each day, for so long I thought there was no hope, I didn't know how I would cope. Many problems I did find While busy searching in my mind, It bothered me to no end But through it all I found a friend. So true to life I pushed him away, never trusting him in any way, He promised to be a constant to me, I was deceived, I couldn't see. He said, walk with me and know my way, I said I'd try but don't make me pray. For I am afraid and I don't trust you. Because I've heard so many others coo Words of love and deep devotion. When it was nothing more than just a motion. How can I trust what I cannot see? He simply said, "Come walk with me". So I went where he led, but not without a fight and he love me anyway in spite of my might. Never once did he ask give your will and be set free, He simply asked me to observe his will for me. Slowly and in all of my dismay, He sent his angels everyday. I came to realize I'd found a friend Willing to be with me until the end, No one else could set me free, No one else would die for me." The commentary on how if you're an S.R.A. and have multiple personality disorder, what a commentary on how hard it is to trust even the Lord and how much more do we need to understand these feelings so we know how to bring these people into healing.

In doing my research for this book, I came across, while dealing with Dr. Don Kaper, a survivor we will call by the name

Sharon to protect her identity. I really felt that her testimony would be good to include in this book as she talks about the healing process and all that she went through. By listening to her testimony, we can gain wisdom and understanding on how to bring S.R.A.M.P.D. into the healing process.

"This testimony does not go into detail or offenses or specific memories of abuse. God wanted all the attention to point to the miracle of His faithfulness and obedience and just enough information for people to understand how broken I was and how He has healed me and brought me into freedom".

"God has called me to share with you today of the miracle that He has done in my life. I feel privileged to be able to do so and I thank you for this opportunity and thank you for helping me be obedient to what the Father has called me to do. There are so many things that the Father has taught me and continues to teach me through this process of healing. I have and continue to experience in my life and in asking the Father what it is that He would have me share with you the response was, I came to heal the sick, cast out demons, and set the captives free and I want you to share how I have done this in your life. I will start with what happened to me and then talk about how it affected me and what my life was like and then will share what was involved in the journey to healing and freedom that God has done in my life. When I was a child, I was a victim of extensive abuse. God separated me in order to survive and what I mean by this is other personalities were created to take part of the pain and suffering

91

so I wouldn't die, because if a person is exposed to too much trauma they can die. This is called Multiple Personality Disorder, aka. DID. The nature of this abuse that I've referred to is called Satanic Ritual Abuse. The many personalities held much of the trauma and each, specific events that fortunately I was protected from so I could carry on with some functional ability. I've been told about all of the personalities and I feel lead to share just a little about two of them. Each of the personalities performed certain functions. For example Damon was the record keeper of the secrets and a harsh overseer of the personalities. After receiving Jesus as his Lord and savior and receiving healing, he chose to take the name of Daniel and had a great love for scripture and shepherded the other personalities. Another is Vicky who is eight and she held the most traumatic memories and had a toughness about her that nobody would hurt her. Following Jesus as her Lord and savior and her healing. She's been given a great gift of discernment for the spiritual realm and a strong desire to obey God at all costs. What this lead to…because of the extensive trauma, I was not only separated into many parts, I also was very wounded. Some things I could identify as problems but I could not figure out why so many things caused me such distress and fear. I developed and eating disorder that was full blow by the time I was 14, which in looking back was among other things, an attempt to remove myself from the trauma and attempt to protect myself as well as something that took a lot of my attention so as not to have to deal with the underlying issues. This was such a strong hold and I sought help for this over and over again and learned how to achieve a superficial level of recovery but the strong hold was never fully removed through these traditional world approaches. I had difficulty attending events or activities where there was a group of people. This included work, social events and church. I also would lose time and at first it was subtle but as time went on it became sever and I did not understand what was happening as I was unaware of these other personalities. I was unable to trust anyone really and when I thought I started to finally be able to trust by friend, Julie, every time we parted, I would have such anxiety about what she thought that I realized I really did not trust, not that I didn't long for trust and security but my ability was just so impaired and this reflected my relationship with God. I also had a severe need to please or appease other people at all costs and would apologize for everything even my very existence. To be touched by others particularly when I was unprepared caused a defensive reaction. This is so much better now but this is one area that God is continuing to heal. Making the littlest decision was a painful process for me. I would often feel depressed, hopeless, anxious. I would worry about everything. I also would get suicidal. God thankfully gave me some level of perseverance and hope, as I would seek out help for these issues. I had counseling from the time I was 16, traditional medical model. I was in two different intensive programs to address the eating disorder and I have been hospitalized on two other occasions actually following coming to know and receive Jesus Christ as my Lord and Savior, to prevent destruction and impulses to kill myself/hurt myself. I have experienced being on medication, anti-depressant, anti-anxiety, and while sometimes those medications assisted in taming some of the symptoms, I never experienced resolution of symptoms and actually for me they numbed me and band aided the bleeding wounds underlying. This is not to say that medication is not helpful and necessary for others because it can be, and sometimes is very necessary, but for my situation it was not the answer. I mentioned that I received Jesus as my Lord and Savior prior to two hospitalizations and I want to tell you about this. I met my friend Ann when I worked at Easter Seals. She got to know me better when she became my supervisor when I was 28. I remember being invited by her to attend the Christian study group Search for Significance at work and I finally went. It was there that I learned for the first time what Jesus did for me, for us and was blown away. It took awhile to understand but with God's help, I began to understand and Ann led me to receive Jesus as my Lord and Savior. It was not long after this that she, discerning all the difficulties I was having, talked to me about healing prayer and her own experience on how Jesus healed some painful things in her life. I remember her asking if I would like to go through this. I said I would think about it and came back a few days later with yes I would like to try. She said she would walk with me through it. Neither of us knew at that point the length or intensity of the journey, which I guess God, knew that it would have been too much at that point; giving us only the information we needed to know at this point. The first time I met with Ann for prayer, I experienced the Holy Spirit for the first time with a flood of memories revealed. There was healing and that is also when the intensity of the spiritual battle began with me not really understanding what happened. It felt like Pandora's box had been opened. In hindsight I recognize it was a demonic reaction, with the Holy Spirit beginning to unveil the darkness within me. I would seek counsel from Julie to understand and she continued to teach me about Jesus and invited me to the church. The Father brought me into a safe community of His body, where I became more comfortable and more prepared as to who He was, before setting me into the greatest intensity. Alice and Father Jame's as well as Ann walked with me through Neil Anderson's 7 Steps to Freedom in Christ, which did help teach me and help me deal with the obvious issues. During that time, there were some very strange things that happened like: me running away suddenly, strong impulses to destroy myself, losing time so severely that I had no memory of one of the days that we were engaging in this, fainting, physical pain that moved through my body. I gave over everything I knew how to and while it did help some, the battle that I did not fully understand how to fight or deal with continued and I felt shame, hopelessness and despair questioning myself of why I was still struggling so and what was I doing wrong. I resigned to the fact that this was my fault and I actually retreated and even started to distance myself from Ann thinking that that way I wouldn't have to face my shame so directly. I did not stop coming to church though being encouraged by Alice and Ann and Father Jame's not to. The loss of time became worse and started really interfering and the destructive tendencies became stronger. I had difficulty reading the Word and would retreat from being around other Christians. I continued to have difficulty suddenly running from church service and many other unusual things happened. Ann and Alison Kidder discerned that there was something more there recognizing that I might need more deliverance and sought help. Dr. Don Kaper, who is highly experienced in the deliverance ministry, as well as being a psychologist and ordained Wesleyan, was recommended by a friend of Alison's and with permission from Father Jame's I met with him following Alison's discussing my situation with him. Father Jame's and Alice were in prayer as was Judy during the time I met with Dr. Don Kaper. Ann and Alison introduced me to Dr. Kaper and it was within seconds after I said hello to him that I fled not understanding why. When I was accompanied back, he explained why, revealing part of the answer to this bizarre behavior that I had experienced for a while reporting that this was a demonic reaction, that the spiritual realm knew who he was and it wasn't me that was running but the demons within me. This explained also why church was very difficult as well as being in the midst of the body discussing the Word as can the Revelations Bible study members attest to when I attempted to attend this study. Other indications of demonic presence included seeing dark image, sensing and actually feeling sudden intense cold all of a sudden. There was confusion and a strong impulse to destroy myself suddenly. It was not unusual for me to feel ill suddenly upon entering church particularly when the word was being read. I would persevere to come to church and there were many time I had to leave the church and actually at times would run out of church and suddenly find myself out of control and at times would have lost time and some one would tell me what happened or be restraining me. Often the impulses were to destroy and if it weren't for the few members of the body of Christ who interceded for me, I would have perished. Communion up until recently caused a demonic reaction in me and sometimes it was all I could do not to scream. Sometimes I couldn't go to church let alone take communion. There was indeed a strong spiritual battle going on within me. The spiritual realm not only consists of demons, which are fallen angels but also the Father's angels. During this process of deliverance and healing, the Father revealed a particular angel that he assigned specifically to me. Being a messenger of God, she brought God's truth, His direction, and His leading to us throughout the healing and deliverance process. In addition, He provided warrior angels to fight (prevail) against the demons. Jesus defeated Satan through His death, burial, and resurrection. However, because of this fallen world, people remain on the battlefield. It is not in their own strength but in the strength of Jesus that the enemy is defeated. The war continues on this earth but it is won for eternity. The start of deliverance and healing. It was during this first meeting with Dr.Kaper that some of the personalities revealed themselves and it was obvious to Dr. Kaper that I was not only demonized but also had multiple personalities. Dr. Kaper, Ann and Alison, while she was here, worked together as a healing team to let the Holy Spirit guide and work through them to help free me and the personalities from demons and heal the memories. Ann and Dr. Don were the vessels He chose to work through throughout this process to bring me the healing He had for me. It was through Ann that the Father restored my ability to trust, to love and be loved as well as how to walk in obedience to Him. And Don who had the knowledge and experience to reveal the truth of the battle and how to cast out the demons in the name of Jesus Christ of Nazareth and bring healing to the personalities. Both Dr. Don and Ann were the vessels that the Father worked through to fulfill His good purposes in my life. One critical factor is that the Father's will would not have been able to be fulfilled in this way had Ann, Dr. Don or myself not been obedient to His call. This was a big sacrifice for Dr. Don and Ann and they are living examples of placing the Father's will first in their life. I struggled with receiving this help, recognizing I needed it but not comfortable with the sacrifice on the part of Ann and Dr. Don Kaper. Julie reminded me that it was about obedience for her, Dr. Don, as well as myself. That by not going forward we would be in disobedience to the Father's will. Those called to this ministry must remember that the Father calls us to be obedient and He will bless those for their obedience. I have been blessed in countless ways, the biggest of which is being set free from the bondage and free in Christ Jesus and Julie was tremendously blessed with the ability to conceive, carry to term, and deliver a beautiful healthy baby. Because of the extensive abuse, there were many memories and many personalities, 55 in all. I was totally separated from these other personalities and the Father directed Dr. Kaper and Ann to lead each of them to Jesus, cast out demons that had resided with them, and He would heal their traumatic memories. This process was quite intensive and extensive and I would have certain emotions and physical memories following a session but not understand them fully because I did not hold the memories. There was layer upon layer of demonic strongholds and traumatic memories and it took a period of two years of intensive spiritual intervention for the deliverance and healing of all the parts of me so that the Father could bring us all together as one. 54 our of 55 of the personalities have been integrated, one remaining to be used for God's specific purposes, one of which is to continue some healing since this is the one I mentioned that has undergone the worst trauma. This is Joy. This process was grueling for all involved. I experienced intense physical pain, as memories were resurfaced, so intense that sometimes I felt like I was going to die. The temptations of the enemy were so great and relentless that I frequently struggled with feeling of hopelessness and giving up. The further I walked down the path to freedom, the greater the attacks of the enemy. I want to clarity something, prior to this clear path the Father provided, I had frequent thoughts of taking my own life out of despair and hopelessness. After I stated on this last leg of the journey to freedom, the two-year period, this decreased but there were more sudden impulses to destroy myself, like a drive. Before there was more conscious thoughts of this but as I started to grasp hold of the truth, I recognized that was not the answer but the impulses that came on suddenly had become more frequent which were demonic in nature. I also want to talk about the eating disorder. As I mentioned earlier, this was something that I struggled with for a long time and understand that it served a purpose for me. The biggest of which as I realize now was to mask the pain and an attempt to cope with all the consequences of the lies I was living. People pleasing vs. God pleasing, worry, blaming myself, living in the framework of deception that I had been taught, taking responsibility for everything that was not mine to take, having an independent spirit rather than a fully dependent spirit on God and an interdependence with the body of Christ, and not fully understanding how to give full Lordship of my life to Jesus, my Lord and Savior. By practicing the eating disorder behavior, which was very destructive, not eating or throwing up what I ate, I was sinning, over and over again. Yes I would ask God for forgiveness and I tried almost everything not to do this. It was a stronghold and the temptation was so great it felt necessary to do this as if I would poison myself or be rejected terribly or just have to feel the pain that was too vast to deal with. Because of the repeated sin I was vulnerable and giving an entryway to Satan, not intentional but definite so it was very hard to break away and I had to do everything it took to stop sinning including continuing this walk on the healing path and feeling the pain that was so intense and calling on the body of Christ and confessing my sin. So sins were committed against me as a child and the nature of the abuse gave entryway to demons, but also my own repeated sin weakened that part of my life that also gave entryway. I think Frances McNutt in his book on <u>Deliverance From Evil Spirits</u> does a very good job of discussing the subject of the possibility of a Christian being able to be demonized and does discuss biblical references. Dr. Don Kaper could also share more on this, but I feel the Father wants me merely to share my own experience to you today. I feel lead to tell you more of what I experienced during the healing. I talked about losing time earlier. This is another thing that became worse during this process. Many others in me were receiving healing and as a result I lost time. It was not unusual for me to be in a conversation with Julie and all of a sudden realize that we had been talking for a long time not even remembering what we talked about. Others were talking to her. I'm so thankful that God gave me the ability to function enough to work during this time. I could not of picked a better group of people to work with and such a loving supportive group. This process was so intense it was all I could do to keep going and He pulled me together enough to do my job. Julie's and my life intertwined a lot through this long period. We work at the same place so she was there and some important duties I had, working with the children as I do. Initially I was fearful of their witnessing difficult situations but as time went on I was able to realize that somehow God was going to use this for good in their lives and they never stopped supporting me, loving me and encouraging me. He also really provided for my children and husband during this time. John through witnessing all that he did experienced God in a very personal way and has come to receive Jesus Christ as his Lord and Savior and has also received some of his own healing. I am blessed to have been given two beautiful, loving children and a loving supportive husband and they were the major reason I kept on persevering through this process. God revealed to me to have Julie share all that was going on with me with the revelations Bible study not too long after I had to stop attending and I have been very blessed by their love, support, and prayers. The Father revealed to me that he cut the old tree down at the very root and has raised up a new tree in me based on His truth. He has been stripping away the old ways and replacing them with His ways and is stripping away the painful memories and freeing me and transforming me into a new creation in Him. It's interesting that around the time of my integration from mid May through June 21, there were literally two trees in close proximity to my home that had things happen. One split right down the middle suddenly for no apparent reason and the other was a huge cottonwood tee in our back yard that was very dead and started dropping limbs that we finally were able to get cut down at the root. The main things I want you to know about today is that we worship an awesome God who is faithful to His promises and wants to heal the broken hearted and set the captives free. Jesus is the Healer and while God can use all things in this world for his good purposes, we must not forget to invite Jesus to light the healing path that he wants to be able to provide for each of us, not looking to this world for the source of our healing but to Him. I want you to know that I had a lot of confusion and deception in regards to who Jesus was as well as religion, church, Jesus was very misrepresented to me early on and if it weren't for God softening my heart and my truth bearers the Holy Spirit, God working through Julie and Don, I would not have really come to know the real Jesus. Satan can masquerade as an angel of light and some of the people who serve him do not appear as evil people. One of the major keys to being set free is forgiving those who have hurt you. This was a very extensive process for me since there was so much bondage and that is an ongoing process of forgiveness as you know, for God calls us to forgive as He forgives us as reflected in the Lord's prayer. The Father asked me to share my testimony with you to give people hope for God's power to heal and set people free. The victory is His. Thought this process, I have learned obedience at all costs. I am understanding the importance of being willing and available to be a vessel through which the Holy Spirit can work through. John 7:37-39, "On the last and greatest day of the feast, Jesus stood up and said in a loud voice, "If anyone is thirsty, let him come to Me and drink. Whoever believes in Me as the scripture has said, streams of living water will flow from within him". By this He meant the spirit whom those who believed in Him were later to receive. I feel the streams of living water are now able to flow more freely within me. Thank you Father. There is victory in Jesus. I'm so thankful for all the support and love that I have received from Holy Spirit Church".

If we are going to bring survivors from S.R.A.M.P.D. into healing one of the things we need to do and know is we need to be able to see things through their eyes. Only then can we be effective in bringing healing to the hurting and the broken. Only then can we have the compassion that we need for them and know the extent of the pain that they have gone through. Every survivor is different, that is why it is good to know their story, good to know what they have gone through, good to know some of the trauma that was involved in them being split and having multiple personalities. Since every survivor is different, every plan for healing will be different. The thing is, God has given us principals we can base the healing on. There are certain principals that can be used with every survivor that is being dealt with, but we must be careful that we don't use things like a ritual. We can't feel as though we have one set plan of healing, for the Holy Spirit knows the heart of man, and the Holy Spirit knows exactly what is needed. Someone needs to be open to the Lord Jesus Christ to know what exactly each survivor needs.

*John Clark PhD*

# CHAPTER SIX

# KEYS TO BREAKING SATANIC
# PROGRAMMING

When dealing with satanic programming one of the key things is to get down to the core of what is going on in a person's life. "Deep in the center of the personality is the core, the fundamental belief that the client holds that are usually not consciously recognized. The client and counselor must use their detective skills to find the deepest core of beliefs". "Each of us has been programmed in his or her unconscious mind to believe that happiness, worth, joy, all the good things of life, depend upon something other than God". Breaking satanic programming

107

cannot be done purely with human understanding or with educational training. In this chapter I will attempt to lay out some guiding principles for breaking satanic programming. I don't want to sound redundant but the one thing I've learned from dealing with this over a period of 400 to 500 hours is that there is no one set formula but there are guiding principles that we can use that will help us to be able to break down satanic programming and the forces of darkness.

In this chapter we will deal with 12 guiding principles in breaking satanic programming and also there will be included some diagrams of Black Widow International Programming so that the reader can get an understanding of some of the depth of some of the satanic programming that is out there, that they can get some type of idea when they start dealing with someone who is SRA and has multiple personality disorder, what they are getting into. Guiding principle #1: The name and the blood of Jesus Christ. Acts 4:12 says, "Salvation is found in no one else for there is no other name under Heaven given to men by which we must be saved". Philippians 2:9-11 says, "Therefore God exalted Him to the highest place and gave Him the name that is above every name that at the name of Jesus every knee shall bow in heaven and in earth and under the earth and every tongue shall confess that Jesus Christ is Lord to the glory of God the father". Colossians 2:14-15 says, "Having cancelled the written code with its regulations that was against us and that stood opposed to us He took it away nailing it to the cross. And having disarmed the powers and authorities He made a public spectacle of them, triumphing over them by the cross". Revelation 12:11, "They overcame him by the blood of the lamb and by the word of their testimony and they did not love their lives so much as to shrink from death". When dealing with satanic programming, it is vital that we depend on the power and the name and the blood of Jesus. The name and the blood of Jesus have so much power that there is no satanic programming that can stand up against the name, power and blood of Christ. After all, the scripture calls Jesus Christ the great physician. It is not us that are doing the work, it is Jesus. So we are dependent upon Him as the great physician to come and help us to finish the work. Guiding principle #2: When dealing with breaking a satanic programming, we are really dependent upon the Holy Spirit's guidance and revelation to get the job done. I John 2:20, 27, "You have an anointing from the Holy One and all of you know the truth as for you the anointing you receive remains in you and you do not need anyone to teach you but as his anointing teaches you about all things and as that anointing is real and not counterfeit, just as it has taught you remain in Him". John 16:13-15, "Though when He, the spirit of truth comes, He will guide you into all truth. He will not speak on His own, He will speak only when He hears and He will tell you what is yet to come. He will bring glory to Me by taking from what is mine and making it known to you. All that belongs to the Father is mine that is why I said the spirit will take from what is mine and make it known to you". I Corinthians 2:9-11, "However as it is written no eye has seen, nor has ear heard nor mind has conceived what God has prepared for those who love Him but God has revealed it to us by His spirit. The spirit searches all things even the deep things of God for who among men knows the thoughts of a man except the man's spirit within him. In the same way no one knows the thoughts of God except the spirit of God". The scripture also calls the Holy Spirit our counselor and when dealing with programming that we don't know much about, we are dependent on the Holy Spirit to show, to reveal, and to guide us into how to break the satanic programming. I'll give you a good example of this. One time we were working with a client and we were working with one particular alter; when we spoke in English to her, the alter was hearing us cuss and blaspheme the name of the Lord. So, what we did was begin speaking in tongues, and speaking in our prayer language to the client and all of a sudden the client was hearing us praise the name of our God. The Jim Smith, he had a word of knowledge that we were dealing with the Tower of Babel Programming. In the Old Testament, that's where God confused the languages, so we said "in the name of the Lord Jesus Christ, we break power of Babel Programming and we command it to be broken" and it was at that point that that program was broken and that particular alter could hear us again in English. She was telling us the story of how when we spoke in tongues, she started to get free, but when we broke the Tower of Babel Programming in the name of Jesus, it totally broke it off of her. So that's a good example of how we need the Holy Spirit's guidance, and revelation to get the job done. Guiding principle #3: We need the power and the word of God to renew the mind and to set the captives free as it relates to S.R.A.M.P.D. and satanic programming. Hebrews 4:12, "For the word of God is living and active sharper than any double edged sword, it penetrates even to the dividing of soul and spirit, joints and marrow it judges the thoughts and the attitude of the heart". Ephesians 5:26, "To make her holy, cleansing her by the washing of the water through the word", 5:27, "To present her to himself as a radiant church without stain or wrinkle or any other blemish, but holy and blameless". Ephesians 6:17, "Take the helmet of salvation and the sword of the spirit which is the word of God". Another good example of the power and the word of God is Matthew 4:1-4 which speak of the temptation of Christ and the scripture says, "When Jesus was led by the spirit into the desert to be tempted by the devil, after fasting 40 days and 40 nights He was hungry. The tempter came to Him and said if you are the Son of God tell these stones to be bread or to become bread. Jesus answered it is written man does not live by bread alone but on every word that comes from the word of God". The word of God is very powerful, it can not only be used to renew the mind and help heal the hurting, it can also be used as a weapon in our hand because Ephesians 6:17 tells us that the word of God is like a sword and the sword is used to fight with, so when we deal with satanic programming, when we deal with alters that need healing, we read them healing scriptures that help in the healing process, and scriptures that talk about how God loves the brokenhearted and those who are downcast. But when we deal with demons that come out in session that want to fight against us, we read the scriptures that tell how Christ had overcome them by and through the cross and how He made a public spectacle of demonic powers and principalities. Scriptures are also used when dealing with satanic programming, when they've been told a lie, for example; when they split the personality in satanic programming, they tell that particular alter that they are their creators, which is a lie because the Bible tells us in Genesis 1:26, "Then God said let us make man in our own image and in our own likeness and let them rule over the fish of the sea, and the birds of the air, over the livestock, over all the earth, over every creature that move along the ground so God created man in His own image, in the image of God He created him, male and female He created them". What we find in session work and in dealing with breaking satanic programming, that it becomes a truth encounter, where the truth of God breaks the lie of the enemy, so using the word of God, knowing how to wield the sword and knowing how to rightly divide the word of God becomes a crucial guiding principle in breaking satanic programming. Guiding principle #4: The gifts of the Holy Spirit and the different anointings in the body of Christ. I Corinthians 12:1,7,12, "Now about spiritual gifts brothers, I do not want you to be ignorant", "Now to each one the manifestation of the spirit is given for the common good"," The body is one unit though it is made up of many parts and though all of its parts are many they all form one body so it is with Christ". We see that there are many different parts in the body of Christ for specific reasons. For example, when we were dealing with satanic programming, The Jim Smith and I, had just really come up against the wall and were really getting nowhere, the Lord gave me a vision, and He showed me a picture. This was like a word of wisdom, a word of knowledge, where it speaks about it in I Corinthians 12. I drew this picture of a bird and kind of a U shaped table with nine chairs and when I drew this room, the client across the table said, "Who showed you that, where'd you get that? You just drew a picture of the satanic ruling counsel of nine in their inner chamber and the bird you drew is the bird called the Phoenix", which we will talk about a little later in this chapter, which was very key in every case we dealt with in breaking satanic programming. Anyway, this is a very good of example of how using and being able to use the gifts of the Holy Spirit in session work is so crucial. Another crucial element we need and are dependent upon is the different anointings in the body of Christ. The Bible says there are many parts in the body and each part has its function, and no one should ever break satanic programming by themselves. You need to go at it as a team approach, and where one brother lacks, another brother will have the gifts and abilities that will help break the programming. Each one has a different anointing in the body and each of us has different functions and it takes a team

113

to do the work. Guiding principle #5: Personal case experience and the experience of others in the same field. There is nothing like personal experience to help out when breaking satanic programming because a lot of the programming is based on similar guiding principles. Also, there's nothing like having other professionals that you know working in the same field, good dedicated Christians that you can go visit with and bring your client to, to further help break the programming. Because we learn from one another, we cannot afford to stay separate in the body of Christ in dealing with those that are survivors of ritual abuse and who have multiple personality disorder. We do not know it all, we are still learning and other people are learning, it's good to get together with what is working. So, the experience of others is of great help. Guiding principle #6: Every case is different and every case for healing will be different depending on the particular client. One of the things you want to be careful with in dealing with satanic programming, everything is done in form and ritual and done with a specific plan. When we as Christians run on a same formula for everybody, it just reminds a survivor of the ritual abuse they just left. So, our plan is just to depend upon the Holy Spirit, the name of Jesus, the blood of Christ, the word of God and all of the other different tools that God has put in our hands to develop a unique plan for every client we deal with. A lot of the guiding principles will remain the same but there never is a specific formula because programming is different depending on what client you are dealing with, how deep they were in the cult and the trauma experiences are different, so we don't have a formula we use for every person, we just have a set of guiding principles. Guiding principle #7: It is God doing the work through us, we don't know it all. We depend upon the power of the Holy Spirit to get the job done and to put the person back together. Zechariah 4:6, "So he said to me this is the word of the Lord to Zerubbabel not by might nor by power but by My spirit saith the Lord almighty". It's very important that we stay humble before God, cover ourselves with the blood of Jesus, and that as we are dealing with people in the cult, that they know that we are not dependent upon our own power, our own strength, our own wisdom to get the job done, but we are doing the work through the power, the blood and the name of Jesus and that we give Him all the glory for the progress that has been made. Guiding principal #8: Education is important but it is only a tool in the hand of God. Do I believe people need to get educated and go to college and get training? Absolutely, because we need education, we need to learn, it can sharpen us and hone us and help us to be a sharp instrument in the hand of the Lord. Just like when pastors go to Bible College, it is good to have Bible training, Bible teaching, Bible activitations so that when you get out in the ministry God can use you to your fullest potential. Guiding principle #9: When breaking satanic programming, it is good to realize and understand how, in the satanic cult, they split the personality and how they do it through trauma. One of the ways they split the personality is through trauma. The following are some examples from my own personal case study of the traumatic things they did to clients when splitting the personality. With one client, they said we want you to learn to astral project, so they threw her in a coffin with a dead body and shut the lid and said "when you can learn to astral project, you can get out of the coffin". Well, this brought her right near the edge of death and eventually she did learn to astral project, but when she came out of the coffin she was highly traumatized. When we took her through this memory, what we found out is that she had died in the coffin, and through Jesus coming, which we talk about in the next chapter, and taking her back into the event, she found out that it was Him who spared her life. But the trauma involved with that memory was incredible, so when her personality split, they did the following. They attached demons to that personality, they gave that personality a name, they gave that personality a function, and they made that personality take vows that they would remain separate for the rest of their life from the other pieces of the personality, and we will deal with that more in the next chapter. Another good example of how they traumatize people is with one particular client, they took her to a ritual and they brought in a body of a young person which they told her was alive, they gave her the sacrificial knife and told her to plunge the knife through the chest, and when she refused to do it, they put the knife in her hand, they raised it up, and they plunged it through the girls chest. Well, this particular client really felt like she killed the person, so when Jesus took her back into the memory, and we took a good look at the memory, we realized that when the knife went in the blood ran out real slow. What they did was deceive her into thinking that she had killed someone, because if the person were alive, the blood would spurt and come out real fast. That same client also took The Jim Smith to the place where it happened and they found the satanic spot, they found the stone altar, and what they did was they desecrated it, they put the alter in the form of a cross, put lilies below the foot of the cross and put scripture over that stone altar, so that they would never come back there again. Another thing they do in satanic programming is they'll put an electrode at the base of the spine and just below the neck and they will begin to run an electric current through it and put the client in a lot of pain until the personality splits. They can then program it, give it a new name, and put the demons in. So, in dealing with breaking satanic programming, it is key to understand how they split the personality, the trauma involved and how they put the demons in, so that when you are dealing with someone who has multiple personalities and who is a survivor of ritual abuse, you know that you need to be careful when dealing with the individual; that you test the spirit. I John 4:1 tells us that we are to test the spirits to see if they are from God. And so it is very, very key that we test the spirits to see if they are demon or human so we don't injure the person or traumatize the person any further. Guiding principle #10: In this chapter we're going to look at, first of all, the inside and outside alarm system that is set up and the extent of the spiritual warfare that goes on when the person is going through the healing process, but also we're going to look at an example of Black Widow International Programming; how it is set up, guiding principles on how to deal with it and how to begin to bring a person with that type of programming into healing. "Hello, My name is Julie. I was involved in over 20 years of Satanism. During that time, I became a high priestess and consort to one who has since become one of the ruling members of the World System and Order of the Phoenix. As such, I was involved in the programming of many of those who have come to be called SRAs (satanic ritual abuse, or survivors of ritual abuse). Having come to a knowledge of The Way, The Truth and The Life that is revealed in and through the word of God and the Lord Jesus Christ of Nazareth, the Messiah, I have become convicted that the knowledge I have a of system programming is something that needs to be shared. I must admit that such a conviction originated from a need to see my own host and counterparts healed and delivered from the programming and strongholds resulting from our life in the Kingdom of Darkness. But in light of the lack of information on programming tactics from an "insider" so to speak, I have come to realize that such knowledge should be shared with all who desire to tear down such strongholds in the lives of those seeking freedom and wholeness. There are many things I can share which will help those involved in ministry to SRAs. There are also things which I could share, but which the Lord has told me to withhold since they would breed dependence upon knowledge, rather than upon a leading of the Holy Spirit. The message He has told me to convey to the reader is that no knowledge of programming, systems, warfare, or hierarchies is a substitute for anointing, humility, and reliance upon the perfect God. It is His desire and mine that what is conveyed here will provide information without that information becoming a substitute for His direction in every situation and counseling session. Many have fallen into deception or error and have made things worse, rather than better, for those they're working with as a result of relying upon their own knowledge and skill. May He grant you wisdom in the application of what you read here and anointing to see the captives set free and the Kingdom of Darkness exposed in this critical hour".

"About the Program Alarm System. When programming individuals through splits and trauma, there are many alarms set-ups as defense against possible threats to that same programming. These alarms are set up with an eye on maintaining control and division, and they are put in place as safeguards with no thought to possible failure. What I mean by that is that programmers are so consumed with pride in their abilities to control and manipulate, that they fail to set up safeguards against the possibility of the alarm system failing! They also give no thought to the possibility that the alarms system or methods of programming will ever be exposed. Pride is the glass jaw that the kingdom of darkness has forged for itself. The alarm system set up to guard programming is set up much like the national defense

119

systems of countries against military or nuclear threat. When a certain conditions is met, and alarm goes off within the programmed systems. This sets defense and refortification strategies into play. If another condition is met, a second alarm goes off, instigating another set of protocols in addition to the existing strategies from the first alarm. For example, if our country detected nuclear build up in China, there would be a general alarm that would put certain safeguards into action, like sending some of our missiles in that direction. If another country, say Russia also powered up their missiles, there would be a second alarm that would initiate safeguard provisions in that area. This second set of defense strategies would be in addition to the strategies already in play from the first alarm. If say an ambassador of our country were slain in one of these two countries, it would initiate another form of alarm and produce another set of safeguards and readiness preparations. This would continue as each condition produced another general alarm or concern until every area of our defense system would be implemented to full operation. We would still be fortifying ourselves on the Chinese and Russian fronts, while implementing more and more protocols for each condition of alarm. Eventually we would be in total readiness against certain confrontation and possible demise. The situation would become more intense with each alarm. The personnel involved in defense would become more and more involved until the activity to protect our way of life would become a frenzy of refortification and defense. Many caregivers of SRAs miss a valuable point in working toward healing with them. Some believe that as work is done in tearing down the systems in SRAs, the host person should be able to more easily maintain or control daily events and attacks. This is not necessarily true. As internal ground is taken, external forces and strategies of defense and refortification will increase! This means that as the host becomes stronger from the healing taking place internally, the forces coming against them increase both internally and externally almost in direct proportion to the strength they've gained. Without understanding this, many caregivers feel the host person is not trying to help in their healing and tend to unwittingly heap condemnation upon the client. Many times the caregivers give up in frustration because of a lack of understanding in this area".

"There are also many strategies built within programming to institute attacks against the caregivers at various stages of alarm. This means that some alarms will set attacks and strategies of assault into action against the caregivers themselves. Unless they understand this, many caregivers fall prey to these strategies instead of standing against them. As I shared this with one minister, he asked what those strategies would look like. I began to answer him with a list of possible events or conditions that would be a sign of attack strategies against the caregiver. But the Lord checked me on revealing that information. I smiled as the Lord spoke that to reveal such things might breed paranoia and reliance upon criteria in recognizing attacks instead of reliance upon His Spirit and wisdom. It is sufficient for caregivers simply to know that there are such strategies and use that knowing to drive them to their knees in constantly seeking God's direction and revelation of when they occur and how to deal with them. The only other key I've been released to give you for recognizing attacks is that they will not only come against you and yours personally, but will also be directed at destroying your relationship with those to whom you minister and with whom you fellowship. In outlining the alarms set up in programming I will note when the strategies of defense go from being primarily internal, to becoming external defenses and threats to the caregivers. In working with your people, if you recognize which state or which alarms are being set off at the time, you may become more sensitive to when attacks against you are most likely to occur as a result of the work being done and the victories being won! This knowledge should be sufficient to help you prepare and increase your seeking the Lord in your ministry and walk, which will inevitably benefit you as much as the ones to whom you minister. Remember, you may be helping others go from strength to strength, but he Lord desires to use all things for all our good. The caregiver should also be going from strength to strength through this process of ministry. That only occurs as the minister continues to rely upon the Holy Spirit and not upon sets of knowledge, regardless of how accurate that knowledge is!"

"The Primary Alarm System. These ten alarms are set in order of occurrence. Some strategies are included which normally occur when each alarm is triggered. Programming is set up so that should no unforeseen scenarios develop, the strategies will be released in direct conjunction with their assigned alarms. Should unforeseen circumstances occur, some strategies may be implemented in earlier stages of healing by order of the external programmers in communication with alters, or by order of Heads of Systems. This outline is meant as a general guideline, not a rigid format. Reliance upon the Holy Spirit is still the caregiver's greatest key to recognizing and dealing with strategies and where your survivors are at in their healing process. Be aware that even as you find yourself in the stage where alarm nine has gone off, all the strategies from alarms one through eight are continuously running. Many caregivers forget that although false Jesus' tend to come into play at alarm three, they are still there at alarm nine, and any alter you're dealing with who hasn't had false Jesus' exposed to them is in bondage to them, just as alters exposed in stages one through three were. And you must remember that unless the alters who have made the decision to go to Jesus have gotten rid of their demons, renounced their vows, and faced the truth of their creation, they cannot fight for the host system. You must be thorough with each alter that surfaces".

"You cannot forget that all strategies going on from the beginning will continue with every alter til the end unless dealt with that alter. This is why often times, caregivers assume the survivor should be able to stand as things get done on the inside.

But the truth is, as ground is taken from the systems, external and internal strategies of opposition against the survivor increase, not decrease! The counter strategies at each level of healing are designed to strengthen attacks against the host system by building upon one another. By the time the survivor reaches level eight, for example, all the counter strikes and strategies outlined below are being thrown at them at once! And these strategies listed here are not an all-encompassing listing!"

We will be looking at ten alarms Condition and Protection Strategies: "1) The outside becomes aware of what is inside. This means that either the person who is out most of the time or companions and caregivers become aware of the existence of others or programs and strongholds within the survivor. Strategy: heads of systems begin to manipulate circumstances to mirror past traumas and continue to bombard underlings with vague memories and emotions, sleep deprivation or disturbances, curse reinforcement, initiation and release of assigned spirits of insanity, fear and denial. 2) Outsiders begin to confront or explore the inside structure or occupants. Strategy: all of the above plus, insiders will begin to surface more frequently to open doorways, demonic strongholds begin to be called upon to bring internal torment, surfacing alters will deny the existence of their own system or other systems, portraying themselves as the only alters present, accusations against possible caregivers will become prominent and trust issues will become stronger, alters masquerading as the host will surface with antagonistic behavior towards the caregivers to deceive the caregivers into believing the person doesn't want help, self condemnation and judgment become a bulwark of guilt and shame to keep the person from believing they can be free. 3) A system is revealed. Strategy: all the above from the first two alarms, plus, the head of that system will cover themselves by having an underling portray themselves as the head, the system will begin to produce false alters to protect their members, one alter will attempt to portray themselves as the core to prevent the true core from being discovered, false Jesus' will become prominent, with them becoming the primary reinforcers of deception and hurts, vow replays become incessant and false confessions reflecting and reinforcing those vows become a more common part of the daily vocabulary, alters with umbilicals and assignments of accessibility to outside programmers will surface and begin making renewed contact with said programmers to reinforce old and receive new programming, belief systems surrounding each alters creation will surface, with the strongest belief that they must be like their creators and were created in the programmers image. 4) On of that system defects. While the host or prominent personality may have made a decision to follow the Lord prior to discovering the contents of the "inside", this alarm will go off when one of those hidden in the now exposed system also makes that decision themselves. Strategy: now you have all the above strategies bombarding your survivor with the additions of: others in the systems will attempt to begin to overload this redeemed one and the host personality with memories and emotions, believing this in itself will destroy that decision, the remaining or resulting new head of that system will begin to also bombard the remaining underlings with the same strategy. This is the only set strategy that will be automatically implemented at this time since the programmers never viewed that making such a decision would remove the alter from the system. The programmers deny the spiritual birth, and hence the transformative power of that decision. Operating on a premise that such a decision is a mental ascent, and not a spiritual transformation, they believe that alters who choose to embrace the "heresy" of Christianity will remain accessible to the system. (To my knowledge, they have never found a way to counteract this new birth and have not been able to develop a new strategy against it, so they continue to use this one although once the alter is removed from the system, it fails to accomplish anything!) The key here is to make sure the now redeemed alter goes to be with Jesus. Do not assume they have. Remember, the new creation is one of faith, and often alters don't believe they can leave the system or they are incapable of doing so because of strongholds, time bombs and land mines. These must often be removed before they can go to safety. Also, remember, the strategy of producing false Jesus' is still in play from alarm three going off. This often causes the now redeemed alter to go with a deceptive spirit or refuse to leave their system out of generalizing fear to the true Lord Jesus unless this assignment is broken over that alter. 5) Another system is revealed. Strategy:

all strategies from alarms one through four continue to run, plus, cross system awareness begins, alters from one systems will begin to influence the alters in other systems to reinforce deceptions and share strongholds. (Sharing strongholds is one area that most caregivers neglect).   Many demonic strongholds will cross systems, making you believe that when you're dealing with say, Mary, and take authority over a demon named Baalfar, that you have irradiated him from the whole person.   In actuality, if Baalfar is a shared demon, you have simply broken his temporary assignment with Mary, while he maintains a stronghold with Sarah in another system. (Commanding any cross system demons to present themselves when binding or casting out demons in dealing with each alter is a key to exposing them and prevents constant ping ponging of demons from one system to another to escape being ousted.   Never cast out a demon unless the alter wants it gone!  They will simply come out and invite it back later with more!  Bind them to give the alter you're dealing with at the time the chance to make a decision for the Lord.  If the alter chooses not to go be with Jesus at that time, then you can also bind the demon to that alter to keep it from moving to another. Binding them to keep them from functioning during a session can be undone by the alter if the alter chooses to participate in the unrighteousness associated with that demon.  But binding them to the alter by the blood of Jesus is not dependent upon the alters actions.  They're stuck with them.  By doing so you guarantee that when the alter is ready for freedom, you will be casting that cross system demon out instead of it's begin able to hid in another system.   Be prepared to find these cross system strongholds present in any system or alter).   Twins, chameleons or impostor programs are implemented to impersonate key members of systems being depleted so that remaining members of those jeopardized systems cannot defect, and hence, at least one alter will remain in those systems to preserve the hope they can be restored.   Caregivers often become deceived or frustrated with this strategy, believing that the alters who had defected have continued to vacillate or have lied to them, will bondages and will worship programs become prominent.   Will worship is where the alters believe they have strongholds as an act of their will. They will often tell caregivers who try to bind their demons that the caregiver cannot do that because it violates their will.   The truth is, caregivers are not violating their will in binding demons, but rather are freeing their will. (This difference should be brought out to the alters as you deal with them and they present this argument).   6) External programmers begin to lose internal control.   Once time has been spent repeatedly confronting some alters with truth, even though they may not yet have made the decision to cross over to the Lord's side, the seeds of that truth will begin to corrode the lies that have become the platform from which the external programmers can exercise control.   Those seeds of truth also begin to become a shield and standard against outside communication, projections, and calling outs of various alters.   Notice I said they begin, not end these activities.   Strategy:

again, all the strategies of defense and attacks against the host from all previous alarms (everything outline above) are continuing!  In addition, at this stage, the following defenses and assaults also join in the fight: manipulating encounters with old associates or other members of satanic orders, hallucinations, false alters masquerade as integrated hosts, an increase in corporate ritual assaults against the host and caregivers. Continuous efforts on behalf of the order (cult programmers) to use superior demonic powers to control or strengthen the remaining demonic strongholds in cult loyal alters, and internal efforts of those same internal demons to reforge or bridge external communications.  Manipulation of external experiences to mimic past experiences of integrated parts.  This causes them to re-split through emotional responses and increases the chance that crossed over, but no integrated alters to return to the system, cult loyal alters will surface and remove, move or destroy things valuable or noticeable to the host person or caregivers, producing depletion of resources, poverty, and confusion, manipulation of non programmer relationships to produce persecution complexes, reinforcement of the internal satanic calendar and clock (accomplished through both internal manipulations and external cues and triggers.  For example, encounters with media about satanic rituals, spotlighting season changes, calendars and elemental cues such as noticing full moons, changing leaves, spring budding, etc.) This is the turning point where external defense strategies of assault against caregivers will begin in full.

129

7) When member so systems cross over so that the number of complete, intact systems is less than the number of depleted ones. Up to this point, all programming and alarms strategies have been geared toward one goal, salvaging or preserving the host and the systems. When the survivor reaches this point, however, all programs and strategies are developed with two possible outcomes in mind. Having reached this stage, programmers realize that it may be necessary to kill the host rather than to try to salvage the host and systems. So the strategies that kick in at this alarm are designed to bring about last-ditch efforts to save the host and systems or destroy them! Strategy: Again, all the other strategies are still running full speed with the following ones beginning with this alarm! Reinforcement of cross system alliances and programs, release of "trump card" time bombs and land mines, physical abduction to create new systems, impart new demonic strongholds, reinforce punishment programs and/or stage scenario productions of programmers becoming saviors from pain or threat, unveiling of and controlled reintroduction of secondary or concealed primary programmers from the past who hold soul ties and strong emotional value to the core personality, or the introduction of false memories of being programmed by currently healthy, supportive relationships. (As I said, the strategies at this level are two fold. With an eye on the possible need to destroy, rather than save the host and systems.) Exposing the secondary or most powerfully emotional programmers is to actually bring about a condition which might set off the next

alarm, (all involved programmers being revealed) such revelation of programmers is used as a last resort and to set the stage for more easily destroying the system should the need arise. The emotional avalanche and identity crises that often result from this unveiling, or from the introduction of deception about healthy relationships the survivor has, will produce one of two possible results. It will either: 1) cause the survivor to respond out of emotional woundedness, thus reopening doors, destroying supportive relationships with those falsely accused of programming them, or resorting to previous splitting behavior to handle the pain. If this does not occur, it will: 2) bring about the quick triggering of the next alarm and set the stage for the strategy of the final alarm, thus speeding up the destruction ultimatum and hopefully preserving some secrets in that accelerated process. In addition to the two possible results to the survivor, this strategy also discredits the caregiver(s). 8) All involved programmers are revealed and exposed. Strategy: Again, all strategies from the first seven alarms now running, with the following being added to the fray: the public exposure of any and all preserved evidence of criminal activities participated in by the host while a member of the order, exposure of any mental incapacity or sinful activities documented about the survivor or caregivers, increased assignments of accusation against the validity of the survivors claims, introduction of infiltrators into the daily relationships of survivor and caregivers, manipulation of any strongholds within the attending church or authoritative and fellowship relationships of the survivor and/or caregivers to sever relationships with coverings and fellow believers, cult loyal alters will begin to integrate one into the other across system lines, to forge fewer, yet more powerful alters to overpower the existing host and manipulate circumstances to tempt the survivor into old habits, initiate cult redeszvous and make last ditch efforts to produce more splits with more demonic strongholds. 9) External programmers lose all external control. Strategy: All other strategies still running from the first eight alarms plus the following assaults: The introduction of non involved programmers within the Kingdom of Darkness, the inclusion of cross order groups in reinforcing all previous strategies. (For example, lets say Paul, Seth, and Warren were members of the OTO and were involved in programming Sally. At this alarm, not only would all the other strategies that kicked in at every alarm up to this point be continuing to run, but now Paul, Seth, and Warren may call in Keith and Grady, satanic priests of WCS, to join them with their demonic powers and influences. These new enforcers would use their superior demons to try to salvage demonic controls still left in Sally's cult loyal alters. They would also do things like have their particular order or group being attacks against Sally's host system and her caregivers. More programmers may be called in for the same reasons from one or more other groups as well. Since only those of the highest ranks within these orders know they are ruled by the World Council of the WWCS, only those of the highest rank would be called in to assist at the triggering of this alarm.) Depending upon the type of programming and level of the individual prior to their leaving their order, such intervention may come from as high up as the World Council itself, with the members of said Council actively using their worldly as well as spiritual positions against the host and caregivers. If one or more members of the Council were originally involved in programming the survivor, other members would be included from the Council to use their particular areas of expertise and strongholds. Increased surveillance of the survivor and caregivers through spiritual and bureaucratic means at the disposal of the new programmers and enforcers, exploration into generational grounds for destruction of future resources or positions the survivor may have been able to achieve if they had never been programmed (robs survivor of hope of normalcy and stability from freedom). 10) Half of those core parts integrate. Strategy: Please notice that each strategy has been heaped upon each previous strategy. By the time this alarm has been triggered, the external and internal forces will both be at peak height and intensity. This stage either becomes the crest from which the survivor will be able to continue on to wholeness or will fall prey to the last strategy of the primary alarm system, which is self destruction and destruction of helpers. One problem with current caregiver strategy is that once reaching this point they assume things are an easy downhill slide. It's at this juncture that many caregivers give up and think that survivor should be standing more than they are able. They fail to see that as the survivor has gained ground, the enemy has release more and more intense strategies against them. If they stand their ground, with caregivers continuing to be a source of strength with them, they will begin to enter the final stages of healing. But be aware, that having survived this alarm system and the resultant strategies will cause a secondary alarm system, instigated by the new (secondary) programmers and enforcers to go into effect. The strategies of this Primary Alarm System will simply be duplicated with the new programmers taking over using them against the integral person (the survivor or host system). This attack against the work already done will then go in addition to the strategies already running to reinforce the remaining cult loyal systems (the strategies we just outlined). This is the last alarm system set in place in programming. There are no other systems because the programmers have nothing else to aim at but the host and the remaining systems. There are no other targets. Over time the survivor will be able to stand stronger like an athlete continuously bench-pressing the same amount of weight each day. They will have reached the limit of the strategies that can be launched against them and will begin to build strength in carrying them and handling them rather than simply maintaining against ever increasing strategies as they were forced to do up to this point. Although good caregivers will always encourage survivors to attempt to do more in their recovery and healing, it is only after these two alarm systems have been exhausted that they should expect the survivor to become increasingly stronger than the attacks. Prior to this, while encouraging more participation, the caregiver should be aware that such increased participation will be by the grace of God and may not meet their desired expectations. Stand against the victim mentality of course! But be aware that it may impossible for the survivor to do more than maintain until all strategies have been destroyed or exhausted. It's because of this area of ignorance that many caregivers and survivors give up just short of the goal. The Lord will guide you in your dealings with these strategies and may give you keys to defeating them. Hallelujah! Rejoice in those victories, but also let your expectations be realistic in light of the onslaught of assault still coming against the work! If you do this, with encouragement and knowledge that the worse it gets, the closer the healing, you won't faint and your survivors won't fall into the trap of condemnation and guilt that often leads them to give up or regress to previous destructive behaviors".

Understanding the alarm systems and everything involved with spiritual attacks and external and internal attacks against the survivor and the caregiver's will give those working with survivors a greater ability to break satanic programming. But another way we can also help in breaking satanic programming is giving examples of programming and in this book I want to include an example of Black Widow International Programming. The following diagram's will help the reader see how the programming is set up, how the system of alters are interconnected, where the core pieces are, and how better to take programming that is built in such a way and see it torn down and to see the survivor brought into healing. At this point take time to look at the following diagrams and after you have looked at them and studied them, there will be comments following to help explain the diagrams.

## Three Dimensional Black Widow Programming

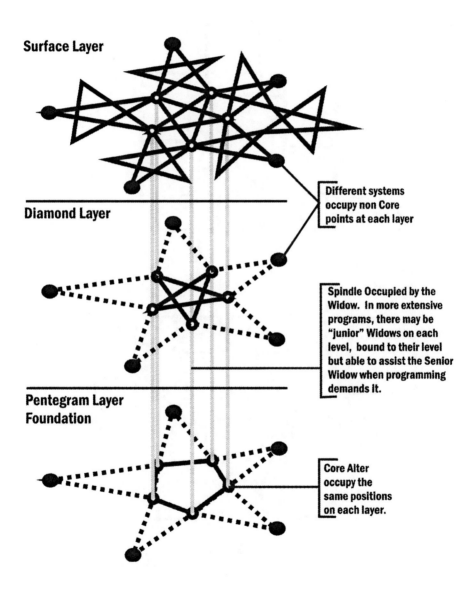

**Surface Layer**

**Diamond Layer**

Different systems occupy non Core points at each layer

Spindle Occupied by the Widow. In more extensive programs, there may be "junior" Widows on each level, bound to their level but able to assist the Senior Widow when programming demands it.

**Pentegram Layer Foundation**

Core Alter occupy the same positions on each layer.

## WEB PROGRAMMING.
## (BLACK WIDOW, INTERNATIONAL PROGRAMMING)
## SURFACE LAYER

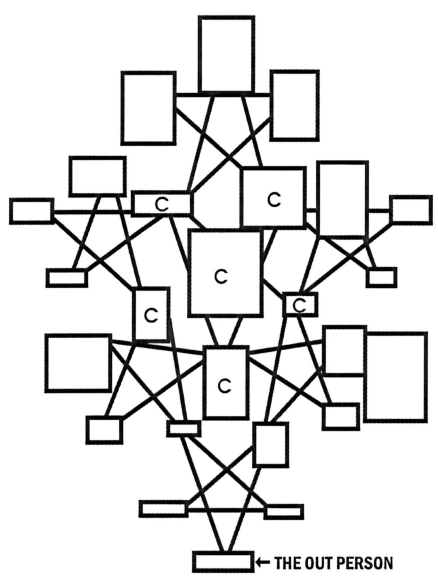

← THE OUT PERSON

**DIAMOND LEVEL**

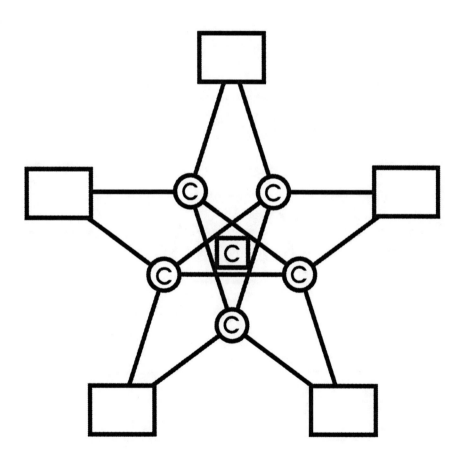

## PENTAGRAM LEVEL

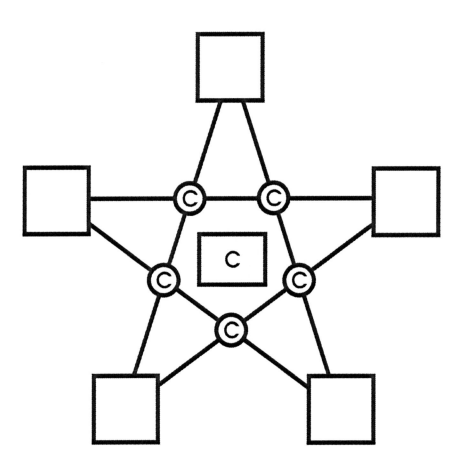

## JEWISH LEVEL &
## SOLOMAN LEVEL

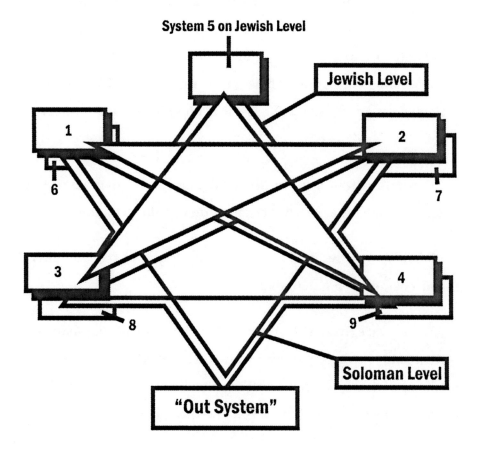

System 5 on Jewish Level

Jewish Level

1

2

6

7

3

4

8

9

Soloman Level

"Out System"

**Systems on both Soloman and Jewish levels
superimposed over each other**

In most every case of Black Widow Programing, the programs are laid in layers. Very rarely is the surface layer the only one present. In such cases where there is no diamond or pentegram programming, then the surface will be the only layer of programs present. One may determine wheather they are dealing with single (two dimensional) layer programming, or 3 D programming once the web is being torn apart. For example, Diamond programming will become evident in one of a number of ways.

1) Alters within a given diamond shape are either fearful or hateful of each other or answer to another in the diamond.

2) There will be double bind martyr programs in the alters found as a point on a diamond.

3) The caregiver will discover that the head of one diamond system may either parceled out their emotions to another diamond systems, or they can feed to or draw from the emotions, emotions, memories and demons of another diamonds heads.

The Spindle is the core shaft upon which the layers are forged. It is ultimately ruled by the Senior Widow, who is, in all cases core or the strongest part of the core. In all cases of 3 D web programming, the core is split intro 6 less portions with the 5 others surrounding the Widow.

The five other parts of the core are not as strong as the widow, but stronger than the other heads and members of the systems. The other 5 core parts will also be able to move from layer to layer by virtue of occupying the outter points of the Senior Widows pentegram. In 3 D web programs, the Senior Widow will have many more in her system than the other system heads.

Some in the downline of the Senior Widow may become junior widows, ruling their assigned layer and having authority over the other Core alters while they are occupying that layer. For example, a Junior Widow may be the ruler of the Diamond layer and have authority over any Core alter also habitating there for a time while another Junior Widow rules the pentegram layer in kind. Both Junior Widows are bound to their layers unless ordered to assist the Senior Widow by the Senior herself, the programmers, or pre-programmed directives. The other five Core alters may ascend or descend the layers, but not at will. They are subject to the Seniors Widows orders and are often ordered to decend if they a are "out" to often, or in danger of having their programing destroyed. Often, When the senior Widow " steps in frount" of another Core part, they will order that Core part Alter to submerge to a lower level. By breaking the Senior Widow and Junior Widow's cord of authority over the Core parts as they emerge in session, and placing them under the protective authority of Jesus Christ, the caregiver can curtail these events. This allows that Core alter to be able to stay surface, to see and hear the rest of the session and take opportunity to either re-emerge later, or choose to be with Jesus on their own. But it is not a permanent measure. If the Core alter chooses not to go be with Jesus, they will place them selves once more under the authority of the Senior Widow, just as Adam chose to step out from under the authority of God in the Garden.

The three layers are imposed one upon the other. With the Core Alters points always hosting the Core Alters or members of there downline on each layer. But the other points of the Diamond and Pentegram layers are habitants of other systems. When viewed from the top down, its impossible to see this. Each layer down holds stronger emotions and memories. Also the alters specific to these two bottom layers have most likely never surfaced since they were split off. They are the most buried and many times, when work in the upper levels is done, their memories and emotions wil begin to trickle into the host or other alters in the surface layer. Most times, the surface alters who are not part of the Core have no idea that layers exist below them and they become subject to overload from these added emotions.

After looking at the Surface Layer of Black Widow Programming, you will notice that it is a series of pentagrams and that each point of a pentagram there is a box, those boxes stand for systems of alters. In each box you could have at least four or five alters at a minimum with a one alter presiding as head over each system. Then you will notice in the middle of the surface layer that the different boxes I have put a letter C in, these boxes stand for core parts. These are alters that are part of the core. In other words, they have memories all the way back to the womb. Then if you look on the surface layer diagram, you will notice at the very bottom you have the out person. This is the person who does most of the daily events, this person and system in that box, is a system design, and programmer's design that we as believers, would never get past that system into the greater part of the programming. So you can see on the surface layer alone, you could have over 100 alters, you can see how it is set up, how they can share knowledge and information and work with one another. Then the next level is the Diamond Level. Once again at the point of the pentagram, you have a box and in this box you have systems of alters. In the center, the circles with the letter C in them stand for core pieces once again. Each core piece has a system of alters even at the new level. Then at the center, you see a box with a C, which is for the Junior Black Widow who is a part of the core and has memories all the way back to the womb. Now Diamond Programming is based on double binds. If you'll look at that pentagram real closely you will see that you can form diamonds. There are at least five diamonds and it is based on double binds. Double bind is when someone is threatened, for example, "if you come to Christ we'll kill your kid", that's a double bind, to help keep them in the cult, through fear and manipulation. Then if you look at the next level, you have the Pentagram Level, and remember, the deeper you go into Black Widow Programming, the more traumatic the memories. And once again, all of the boxes and the circles have systems of alters,

145

new systems of alters at every level. Then you have the Jewish Level and the Seal of Solomon. When we were working with Black Widow Programming, we even got to a point where we uncovered a self-destruct plate. When you get that deep in the programming there are systems of alters that come out, who their function is to destroy the body. Now when working with Black Widow Programming, one of the keys is when one of the core pieces get to know Jesus, that core piece can, on behalf of all the other pieces connected to it, break vows on their behalf and really can accept them and integrate them into themselves. When core pieces come to know Jesus, a lot of the ones that broke away from them or broke off of them, Jesus will bring them back to them and they will come to know Jesus and integrate, this really speeds up the process. But, this example of Black Widow Programming is just, and I cannot go into all the explanation of it, it's just an example to help someone who is working with satanic programming, knowing how it is set up and how to better tear it down.

Guiding principle #11: Expect the unexpected. When working with satanic programming and breaking satanic programming, we need to expect the unexpected. Remember there is no set path; there is no set formula in doing this. One of the things we ran into that I did not expect, is that there were some alters that felt they were part demon and because they felt they were part demon, they felt they could never come to Christ. So what we had Jesus do, we had Jesus separate the demon from the human part of the personality and then that part of the personality could see that they were not evil and that they could receive Christ. So, you always need to have your mind open, the enemy could try to throw a twist in the midst of breaking the programming. So that is where we are really dependent on the Holy Spirit to give guidance and revelation. Guiding Principle #12: Always keep your eyes on Jesus and do not be impressed with the darkness. Hebrews 12:1-3, "Therefore since we are surrounded by such a great a cloud of witnesses let us throw off everything that hinders and the sin that so easily entangles and let us run the race of perseverance the race that is marked out for us, let us fix our eyes on Jesus, the author and perfector of our faith, who will further joy before Him and endured the cross its scorning and its shame and sat down on the right hand of the throne of God consider Him who endured such opposition from sinful men so that you will not grow weary and lose heart". We must remember to keep our eyes fixed on Jesus, it is not our job, it is not our power, it is not our strength, it is not our wisdom that enables to break satanic programming, it is Jesus. Jesus is both the beginning of the healing process and the ending of the process. And He is in the middle of the process, so we are utterly dependent upon Him for help, to know how to do this I would say the biggest and the largest key of all, the largest guiding principle of all, is stay close to Jesus and do whatever He says.

# CHAPTER SEVEN

# SESSION WORK, HEALING AND HEALTHY INTEGRATION

This chapter will be based on a lot of my own personal experience with session work, healing and healthy integration because I have found that with over 400 to 500 hours of working in this field that all three of these happen at the same time. When having a session, we also need to be praying for God's healing to be poured into the person's life. It's during the session time, most often, when different parts of the personality will come out and get cleaned up and go to be with Jesus. Not only to be with Jesus, but they will integrate back into the personality where the Lord would have them to go. So this chapter will be some guiding principles on how session work happens, what happens in session, how healing comes about, and the process of healthy integration. I'm going to share with you some things you need to do before you do a session and then what happens during a session, all the way from the healing process, to seeing a part of the personality set free, to seeing also the part of the personality integrating, and a part of the host. Because basically, that same process happens with every part of the personality you deal with, so what I want to do is take you from the beginning to the end, including the dealing with the demons and how we have dealt with them, in a way without seeing the part of the person itself more traumatized in the process. The following are the steps that we use before we enter a session all the way through to seeing a part of the personality receive Christ as their savior, to going to be with Him, to coming back and integrating and becoming a part of the personality where God designed that part to be. I haven broken the process down, step by step into 39 steps. This is not an exact plan or a formula, these are only principles that will help guide the reader in helping someone who is a survivor of satanic ritual abuse and who has multiple personality disorder into healing. The following is Step #1: Preparation. It is always good before you start session work to have people praying and fasting for you, and it's also good to fast yourself. Enlist a team of intercessors to be praying for you on the day you are going to be having the session.  Get as many people, with prayer and intercession in the body of Christ for you as possible, because then you'll have the greater breakthroughs when working with the different programming and with the different obstacles that come up before you during session.  Step #2: Find a safe place to meet every week.  A good safe place would be like a church.  Meet at the same place every week because that will make the survivor more comfortable.  Step #3: Never do session work by yourself. There should be at least two or three people working together in the session because it takes the different anointings in the body of Christ to be successful in bringing these people into healing. When one is working with a survivor, the other ones can be praying and vise versa.  This helps for a greater breakthrough.  I also want to say at this point, those that start to do session work and are involved with a survivor in the healing work, need to be prepared to stay in it for the long haul and not the short sprint. The survivor needs to know that the person working is committed to their healing and to see them healed.  Step #4: It is good to remember that there is no set plan or expectations for the session except for allowing the Holy Spirit to lead and guide the session. "The treatment of the insane is one of the most important questions connected with the subject of fait.  In my experience in dealing with cases of insanity, there isn't one set pattern you can follow.  But there is one thing we must remember: the true remedy for all deliverance, from sin, sickness, from demons, or from any evil, is the power of Jesus Christ".  Step #5: The host must want his or her own healing and must be willing to face problems and the truth about situations that have happened in his or her own life. "There are several steps that a person can take in order to resolve a crisis situation in their life. First of all, it is important to recognize that there are solutions to any crisis. In order to solve a crisis you must be willing to face the problem. James 5:16, in many ways, talks about the need to facts the truth about a situation". If the survivor is unwilling to face the truth about the situation in his or her own life or is not willing to also pay the price to come into healing, then the survivor can never be healed. Step #6: The survivor should have a church home and other people who can pray with him or her on a weekly basis. There will be a time when there will be a great need for others to do spiritual warfare on their behalf. So, having a church home and having other people who can pray with the survivor is a great help in the healing process. This means being willing to get a phone call at anytime of the day or night, if that survivor needs a prayer, that it's okay to call, it doesn't matter if it's 3:00 a.m. in the morning. Step #7: The survivor must be willing to renounce the kingdom of darkness and all of its works. Renouncing the kingdom of darkness is key to being set free. The following is a good prayer of denouncing the kingdom of darkness and affirmation of the Lord, Jesus Christ. "I confess and repent of all my sins which have given ground to Satan and his forces at any time in any way, in any and all parts of my being. As a child of God, purchased by the blood of the Lord Jesus Christ, I here and now renounce and repudiate all the sins of my ancestors. As one who has been delivered from the power of darkness and translated into the kingdom of God's dear Son, I cancel in the Name of the Lord Jesus all demonic working, which has been passed on to me from my ancestors. In Jesus's holy name I cancel any demonic working upon me through any other person and likewise cut off by the finger of God any psychic force from any person whatsoever from working on me, in me or through me. I cancel in the Name of the Lord Jesus Christ any ground I or others have given, concerning all aspects of my being, to Satan and his forces at any time in any way. I forgive all others, as I want God to forgive me. As one who has been crucified with Jesus Christ and raised up to walk in newness of life, I cancel in the Name of the Lord Jesus Christ every curse that has been put upon me. I announce to Satan and all his forces that Christ became a curse for me when He hung upon the cross. As one who has been crucified and raised with Christ and now sits with Him in heavenly places, I renounce in the Name of the lord Jesus Christ any and every way in which Satan and his forces may claim ownership of any and all parts of me. I declare myself to be completely and eternally signed over and committed to the Lord Jesus Christ. I renounce Satan and all his works, and I confess Jesus Christ as my Savior, Lord and Master. I choose that Jesus Christ is Lord of my entire being, and any and all aspects of my being, and with all that is within me, I bless His Holy Name. All of this I do in the Name and Authority of the Lord Jesus Christ, applying all of this to myself and all aspects of my being." Have these prayers written out and photocopied so that the survivor can take them home with him or her, so that they can read them in their time when they feel they are under attack by the enemy. Step #8: The survivor should be taught about the importance of forgiveness and what it means to forgive. "Forgiveness is the principal thing needed to pave the way for freedom. As long as unforgiveness is present, God's hand of protection, mercy, and restoration is hindered at best, and stopped at worst. Forgiveness, though often the hardest part of the counseling process for the counselee, is the prerequisite for lasting healing". The counseling must be taught but forgiveness isn't something we can do, it is something that God does through us. Forgiveness is an act of the will, not just an emotion, it really depends on God to give us the power once we yield our wills to Him to help us forgive the people that have so greatly hurt us. Step #9: Everything that happens in session must be based on God's word because even in the Christian world today, I have noticed that there a lot of areas where the new age practices are coming in. Even things like hypnosis and many other new age practices are trying to come into the Christian circles and Christian counseling, so, it is good to know the word and to know that you are dealing with something that is not biblical. Step #10: Before you do session work it is key to understand the legend of the phoenix and the spirit that is behind it, as it relates to the healing of someone who has been satanically ritually abused and has multiple personality disorder, because the spirit of the phoenix must be bound in the name of Jesus before any session starts, and you should bind that spirit with every alter you deal with. The legend of the phoenix is as follows: "The phoenix is a bird from ancient Greek, Egyptian and Arabian mythology that lived in Arabia and was sacred to or a servant of the sun god of ancient Egypt. The phoenix is described as a heron in Egypt, but is usually depicted as a peacock or eagle like bird with red and gold plumage. Only one phoenix could exist at one time and every 500 or 1461 years when it felt it's end coming the phoenix would build a nest to be used as a funeral pyre. The old phoenix is then consumed in flames and burned to ashes. A new phoenix would then rise from the funeral pyre. This process is said to symbolize the rising and setting of the sun. After embalming the ashes of it's predecessor in an egg of myrrh it would then fly with it to the City of the Sun and place it on the alter of the sun god. The phoenix symbolizes immortality, resurrection and life after death. Depictions of a phoenix have appeared in Egyptian, Greek, Hindu and Chinese art and writings for a very long time. It also later appeared in medieval Christian writings as a symbol of death and resurrection. Its flight has been said to represent the capacity to leave the world and its problems behind, flying towards the sun in clear pure skies". The reason understanding the legend of the phoenix is so important, is because the ruling counsel of the Satanic World's Church, the ruling counsels coat of arms is the symbol of the phoenix and the reason this is so important, is that when people are ritually abused and programmed, they are put on the altars, they are tortured until the personality splits, they are told that they are a part of the phoenix. They are told that out of the ashes of the old person was created a new person and that they can never go back, they can never face the truth about what happened to them, that they are part of the phoenix, that they have to keep flying away and that they can never go back in and if they do go back in with Jesus and face the truth, that they will die. This is so important, because in ritual abuse, out of the fire of abuse, the new person arises; this is what the world counsel does when it programs people. It abuses people to the point that they try to put to death the old person, the person made in God's image, and out of that old person, comes a new person created in their image, in fact the programmers tell people they are abusing that they are their creators, that they created them, and this is the lie that they try to put in the minds of those that have suffered ritual abuse. But we know according to Genesis 1:26, "Then God said let us make man in our own image and our own likeness and let them rule over the fish of the sea and the birds of the air and over the livestock and over all the earth, over every creature that moves along the ground", "God created man in His own image, in the image of God He created him, male and female He created them", and Psalms 139, we know the scripture says that God knit us together in our mother's womb. So this is one area that people working with those that have been programmed from the satanic kingdom will have to fight against. This truth will have to be one of the first truths that an alter understands, this is where Jesus coming and taking them back to face the truth comes in. Here is where you really need to pray and intercede for the part of the person that you are dealing with, because they will be very afraid to go back and face the truth, for fear that they will die; for fear of the great punishment that will come upon them. Step #11: Pray before you start the session off. It's always good to do the following: Pray and bind Satan and apply the blood of Jesus to everybody involved in the session, to all the intercessors, all the families involved, to the survivor's family. Pray that the Holy Spirit would lead the session and ask Jesus to bring out the part of the personality that He wants you to deal with. Don't think that you know what you are going to do, leave it all up to the Lord, and remember that every alter that comes out will have a name, every name will have a meaning, and every alter has a function or a job that they feel they need to be doing. For example, an alter could be named Satyr, which meaning is the worship of false gods and that would be very important understanding the function of that particular alter and how to pray for them. Also remember the alter themselves will not want to give up the meaning of its name or function of their job or what they have been programmed to do, so you really have to listen, pray, and ask for God's understanding. Step #12: When a personality comes out it is at this point where you must test the spirit. I John 4:1, "Dear friends do not believe every spirit, but test the spirits to see whether they are from God because many false prophets have gone out into the world". It's very important at this point that the human is separated from the demon, you do not want to treat part of the personality as a demon and you don't want to treat a demon as part of the personality. One of the tests we do when working is session, say "in the name of the Lord Jesus Christ who can't come in the flesh, I command you to tell me are you human or are you demon?" Because, we tell them if they're human we don't want to treat you as a demon but if you are a demon, we're going to cast you out. And so, at this point, it's really good to go ahead very carefully and test the spirit to make sure that you are truly and genuinely dealing with a part of the personality. Because, I have had it at times where we were dealing with personalities, and we were talking with one for a long time, and all of a sudden realized we weren't talking with part of the person, we were really talking with a demon and so we bound it at that point. It's also good when the different personality parts come out that you cut off all spiritual chords connected to the people they call their creators, or the ones who programmed them, and totally separate them from their programmers or their creators as they would call them. At this point you must have a lot of discernment. Step #13: When a different part of the personality comes out, bind the demons that are connected with them or that have been programmed to them, bind the demons that are with them and to them, in the name of Jesus. Not in a way that would hurt them, but in a way that would enable them to hear and see truth. Also bind the power of the phoenix, bind all demons to that system so that they cannot cross to any other systems in the programming. Ask the Lord to send in His Holy angels to guard, to protect and to minister, but the demonic spirits that stand in the way of that part of the personality coming to Christ, must be bound and also gag them in Jesus's name. Step #14: Ask the part of the personality that is out if they know why they are out and then just wait, and a lot of times they'll say "I didn't want to but I got pushed out here". You can share with them how Jesus brought them out and there's something that the Lord wants them to see and there's some truth that He wants to show them. Step #15: Remember that survivors who have multiple personality disorder see things on the inside, they can see the other personalities that are on the inside, they can see Jesus on the inside, so it's also very important that you bind all false christ's that would want to come and interfere with the session because Jesus is not necessarily a positive word with the different parts of the personality because in ritual abuse, they dress people up like Christ to abuse the people that they are programming so the word and the name Jesus and the thought of Jesus would repel them from Him instead of draw them to Him. So sometimes when you are in session work with a survivor, you'll see them with their eyes closed but you can see their eyelids moving like they're watching a movie screen. That's because they see everything in color on the inside and there's a whole different world on the inside that you and I are not even aware of and we can't really relate to. Step #16: Ask if you could pray for the alter who is out talking to you. **Pray for Jesus to come and reveal truth and to reveal to them why they are out and what he wants them to see. This will be greatly resisted by the alter because they are told they can never go back and look at the truth. Step #17: After you have asked for Jesus to come and reveal what He wants to reveal to them, then wait. Wait on Jesus to come, you will see the alter's eyes moving and they will move back and forth, like I said before, like they're watching a movie screen. Step #18: Ask them what they are seeing. Don't suggest anything, don't use guided imagery, and don't put thoughts in there that aren't there. Ask them what they are seeing and if you don't understand something they are seeing, ask them to explain further what they are seeing, so you know clearly what they are seeing. It's amazing, now this is not hypnosis, they are in full control of their personality and will, they are seeing things on the inside as Jesus reveals it to them. At first when they see Jesus coming to them on the inside it'll really frighten them and you have to pray and encourage them that it's okay. This is the true Jesus, He won't hurt you, He loves you. Step #19: It is at this point often times, demons come out and try to interrupt the session. When this happens, we take the head demon and we chain him to all the other demons and all the other shared spirits that are below him and above him and including, binding him to Satan, then we asked the angels to come and to take the demons away, to put them where Jesus would have them to go. Step #20: When you are dealing with a part of the personality that is out, encourage them to trust Jesus. To look** into His heart, to see His kindness and His goodness, to accept Him as their savior, and to go with Him and to see the truth and to see the things that He wants them to see.  It's also good to pray that Jesus would separate false memories and things that weren't real from the things that are real so that the alter has a very clear understanding of what they have gone through.  There are times when there will be misleading and there will be false memories that have been implanted in the alter's mind.  Step #21: Ask Jesus if there are other parts that He might want to bring back to integrate with this particular alter; because some times the alters have split off parts that have to do with their emotions so they don't have to deal with their emotions.  Often times Jesus will bring that and integrate back with them two or three other parts that they need, that they've split off, that they need to have joined to them so that they can see and understand the truth that Jesus wants to reveal to them in a complete manner.  Also remember this will be resisted by the alter because they are told that integration is very bad.  Step #22: During this time, ask that Jesus' healing balm would be poured into the survivor's wounds and that Jesus would continue to pour in His healing oil during the session so that as memories, and as things that are coming out that are very hard to deal with, that the healing process can begin right then.  Step #23: When parts go to be with Jesus, they often come back with a new name and a new job that Jesus would like them to do and their names have particular meanings.  It's good to mark what those meanings are.  But at this point, I want the reader to also understand when a part goes to be with Jesus, sometimes you don't see or hear from them for two or three days or even two weeks.  When they come back they will address themselves to you with a new name but they will tell you what they formerly were and they will be excited about the new things that Jesus wants them to do.  We are going to go on in these steps as if there wasn't a break in the process, but remember usually at this point; there is a break in the process.  That is why it is good to keep good notes to know who has broken vows and who hasn't, who's integrated and who hasn't integrated and what the new names are.  It's also good in the note keeping and in the record keeping because what happens is, you will be able to put the alters in systems, you will find out who heads of systems are, and the programming specifically that you are dealing with will begin to take shape, you will begin to understand how to set up, and the Lord will show you and give you the keys to take it down.  Step #24: Remember that when dealing with part of the personality and seeing a personality go to Jesus, you will be dealing with a lot of trauma.  During this time, when the trauma is going on, while one is doing the session work, it's always good for another one to be reading scriptures that have to do with healing and comfort.  And also, in sessions, you will be dealing with a lot of double binds.  A double bind is when part of the personality is told that if they ever come to Christ one of their kids on the outside will be killed or someone on the inside will die, this brings a lot of fear, and the satanic kingdom is built on a lot of fear and manipulation.

When you overcome the lie with the truth, the house of cards will begin to crumble faster and faster, and the programming will begin to break down quicker and quicker. Step #25: If the part you are dealing with is a core part and has memories all the way back to the womb, a lot of times they have a lot more trauma. But when they come to Jesus, a lot of times, a whole system will want to go to be with Jesus with them. But remember that core parts can break vows on behalf of the other ones that were split off of them, and so if they want, they can also bring back to them the parts that were split off of them; you can see a whole system integrate together and go to be with Jesus all at once. I just wanted to put this information in at this point because this is so key, because if you have a Junior Black Widow go to be with Jesus, that Junior Black Widow can break the vows on behalf of all the other ones that were split off of it and also, like in the Black Widow Programming a Junior Black Widow can, like say, run the whole Diamond Level, and we have seen whole levels of programming and alters go to be with Jesus almost all at once and literally cause a spiritual earthquake to the whole system of satanic programming that was set up. It is good to remember this information. It could be very helpful when dealing with alters and the healing process. Step #26: At this point, when an alter goes to be with Jesus, most always there will be another alter that will pop right up, Jesus will shove them right up front to talk with you, so you want to keep your eyes open and keep alert, and awake and recognize switches. Watch the eyes and listen to the voice, because a lot of times the other alters will want to try to fool you. So remember, when one alter goes to be with Jesus they don't normally come back right away, normally another one comes out that the Lord wants you to deal with. Step #27: When a part comes out that has been with Jesus, with a new name, the next thing they need to do is break the vows they took and all the pacts and agreements they had with the cult. Ask Jesus to reveal the vows they are to break. Usually the first vow is they make a vow to forget their vows. This will almost always be the first vow that comes up. This also could be the point where the demons surface. Sometimes the demons surface before they go to be with Jesus and sometimes they surface after they come back out with a new name, and they break the vows and the demons come out during the time when they are breaking their vows. So, you want to remember that when dealing with an alter who has a new name but hasn't broke their vows, this is very key. Step #28: After all vows are broken and all demons are removed and gone, it's at this point that they are ready for integration. What I mean by that is, there is nothing that can stop them now from integrating, but sometimes Jesus doesn't integrate them right away. Integration is really up to the Lord and only He can put them back where He created them to be in the first place. Step #29: Integration is up to Jesus. When it's time, Jesus will integrate them where He wants them to be. For healthy integration, all vows must be broken and all demons must be removed and that personality must be cleansed by the blood of Jesus for the integration to be healthy. Step #30: Sometimes integration will happen without vows being broken. Sometimes Jesus will integrate a particular alter into another alter. For example, say the alter's name is Sally, the host name is Sally, and Jimmy or Jackie integrates into Sally, but Jackie hasn't broken her vows, because she integrated into Sally, Jackie's vows now become Sally's vows, and Jackie's demons now become Sally's demons and the vows need to be broken again and the demons need to be removed. This is key in keeping the host healthy and strong. Every session the prayer should be "Lord, are there any more vows that the host personality needs to break"? The constant breaking of vows is key in keeping the host healthy and strong. Step #31: After integration, the host will have to deal with the new memories from the parts that have integrated into the host. This can be very hard to deal with because the memories and the things that happened and the things that they have done, they have to own for themselves. Because really, it is one person with many personalities and anything done by the particular person, they all have to own. Step #32: Remember to ask the Lord to give you the keys to taking whole systems and levels of programming down at once to go to be with Jesus. Sometimes we have seen up to 10 to 20 alters go to be with Jesus all at once. I believe there is much to be learned in this area and that the Lord wants to speed up the healing process. But, we must be sensitive to the Lord and the leading of the Holy Spirit to know what to do and what not to do. Indeed, Jesus does hold the keys to the kingdom of Heaven and

He has overcome hell, death and the grave. Step #33: Remember also that little ones will come out and will want to go to be with Jesus, but when you have one little one talking to you, normally there is a whole group of little ones that are there who haven't taken any vows, who haven't been programmed, and often times they go to be with Jesus, all at once, He takes good care of them, and when they come back, they don't all necessarily have new names, they just all go and integrate. But, they have no vows and so their integration affects the host in a good way. It does not affect the host in a negative way, like someone integrating that still has vows and demons. It's also good to remember that you often deal with people that they call on the inside "crack" people. These are splits in the personality that haven't been programmed, that haven't been used yet, that can be used if a system disappears, because what the cult will do after a system has gone to be with Jesus and has been removed, if they can abduct that person and reprogram they will try to replace that system with another system. Step #34: As integration happens, more and more, when you get to the end of the programming you will find what we call the "birth" person. Under all the programming is really buried the birth person. That is the person that they don't want you to find. At the end, the host will integrate into the birth person and the person you have will be whole. But, as you get to the end of the programming, you will begin to discover the names of the people and the programmers, of what the real names are, and what the birth person's real name is. Often, that is disguised, often the person you are dealing with, and their name is not their real name. The satanic cult will often raise their own children and they do things their own way. Step #35: Watch out for false integration to try to get you to stop the work and make you think the work is finished. One of the ways I found healthy in testing is to anoint and laying on of hands and begin to pray for God to come reveal that the work is really done. When we have done this before, what happened was, there was an integration but a lot of the darks ones integrated and tried to portray themselves as an alter who had gone to be with Jesus. They tried to portray themselves as the host, like the host was totally integrated. But as we laid hands and prayed, there was an alter that was standing in the way trying to pretend, but the host was allowed to come back out and the healing process continued. Step #36: Only Jesus can test the work to see if integration is truly complete. Ask Jesus to test the work and wait to see what happens. Watch the eyes closely, watch for switches. I had a lady who came in my office and said she was completely integrated and I said, "if I throw out some trigger words they won't bother you, hu?" When I threw out some trigger words she began to switch and I called her back and stopped the switching from happening. I've yet to see or find or hear about an alter who is totally 100% integrated. A couple of the survivors that wrote for my book, still have a couple of personalities left but when they have over 500 and they go down to less than 50 or less than 10, you have done a lot of work, but the work is a long process. Step #37: Always give all the glory to

Jesus and stay balanced with your family. Don't let the work of ministry and deliverance consume you. Don't become unbalanced. Remember it takes a team to take care of a survivor. Step #38: The survivor will need your prayers the rest of his or her life. They will become a part of your team eventually and also help others in the healing process. Step #39: It is good to note if you are planning to expose the cult and call the police on things that you have found, make sure you have your facts straight. For example, one of the cults ploys, when people turn their back and want to testify against them, is to get the survivor on the stand and then send in their own psychologist into the court room to throw out some trigger words to trigger their multiplicity on the stand so that the survivor will be seen as being incompetent. Most often the things that the cult does, they don't use real names, no one uses their own name, and if they kill somebody, they often cremate them or they send in cleaners to use acid to dissolve the body and the bones so that there is no evidence of human parts left or remaining. In one case, one of our survivors was abducted and they took her to a place up near Big Lake, Ohio. This is the place mentioned earlier, where she took my friend, The Lords Messenger, and found the stone altar and the ritual spot. This is where they put the altar in the form of a cross, put lilies on it and put a scripture all over it to desecrate it because once you desecrate one of their spots they will not return to that spot. Remember, it's dangerous to go to a spot by yourself because normally they have people watching those spots. Also, you and I should never walk into the enemies fortress thinking we can do it all ourselves. We are only to do that which Jesus has assigned us to do. We do not chase demons, we do not try to invade ritualistic meetings, we just ask the Lord to do the work, and we ask the Lord to send His light and truth into those meetings. We ask Jesus to reveal to these people salvation so that they might be saved and become a part of the kingdom of God, because Jesus loves these people just as much as you and I. In closing I want to say in this chapter that, during the session you may have some guiding principles but always expect the unexpected. You are going to be dependent on Jesus to give you the wisdom to know how to deal with the memories, traumas, demons, forgiveness and the word. There is so much that you will be dealing with, if you just keep your eyes on Jesus and listen to the Holy Spirit and stay humble, the Lord will help you make it through because God uses normal people to do the extra ordinary things. So many things happen during a session that if I were to write every detail of everything that we saw happening in session, there would be pages and pages of detail but I believe that every client is different, every person is different, every program is different, every abuse and trauma and split is different. We need to depend upon God but it is always good to have the guiding principles and knowledge of others that have worked in the same field.

# CHAPTER EIGHT

# KEEPING GOOD MENTAL HEALTH IN THE HEALING PROCESS

Probably the major aspect of this chapter is keeping the survivor healthy during the healing process. You know even more important than tearing down strongholds and destroying satanic programming and seeing alters integrate is if you're going to have four hours of session work a week, you're also going to need at least eight hours of counseling a week that will offset the session work being done. Now the only problem with this is that most survivors of ritual abuse come out of the cult with absolutely nothing, with only the shirt on their back and so it's probably a really good idea during this time that the survivor be hooked into a local church, be a part of a local fellowship, be part of a cell group in a local fellowship, be involved as much as he or she can with the fellowship because a lot of times being involved in the church body you have people who attend who are doctors, nurses, psychologists. Maybe some of them would be willing to donate their time to help with psychological counseling aspect of the healing process, because it is a big aspect. Most survivors will tell you the big thing they need after session work is someone to talk to, someone to counsel with, and it doesn't necessarily have to be professional counseling, it could be just someone within a local church that is working with people like this and understand a little bit, who are just willing to sit and listen to this person explain what they are feeling and to pray for them because the psychological aspect of this whole thing is incredible; the amount of pain and trauma that a survivor goes through. Chris Thurman gives the twelve best secrets for living an emotionally healthy life and they are: "1) The absolute necessity of truth for an emotionally healthy life; 2) To err is human. You've heard it all of your life, to err is human to forgive is divine, sure you've heard it, but I would be willing to bet you don't really believe it that making mistakes is normal, my guess is that you go on each day trying to be perfect or semi perfect and then feel disappointed if not outright annoyed whenever you make a mistake; 3) What should have happened did. Using should is our way of saying we don't like the reality we face. Should represents the unwillingness on our part to deal with reality as it is; 4) You can't please everyone. You can't please everyone line is one of the greatest truths we need to recognize and practice in order to lead emotionally healthy lives; 5) You don't have to. You don't have to be a cannibal to be fed up with people; 6) You are going to die. This may be a terrible truth but it is the truth that can be used positively to prompt us to live a life more fully; 7) The virtue lies in the struggle, not the prize. One of the great ironies of life is that people complain constantly how hard it is to get ahead, yet when they no longer have to struggle they seem eager to go stir crazy and make work for themselves or they lose their inner sense of purpose in life and develop emotional problems; 8) You are not entitled. One of the most difficult attitude problems any counselor can face is that of entitlement. Entitlement is an attitude of I'm owed, it is apparent in beliefs such as these; I'm a college graduate so I deserve high paying jobs, I've been good to my friends so they owe me their loyalty; 9) There is no gain without pain. Imagine your reaction what it might be if you saw the feature staring you in your hometown newspaper tomorrow morning that read as follows: New psychosurgery technique developed. Personal maturity now possible without any effort; 10) Your childhood isn't over. A fair number of people see the past as something that is over and done, it needs to be forgotten or left behind, yet it isn't quite that easy is it? As much as may seem like a self indulgent waste of time to look backward in time, our own unique history often demands to be examined and dealt with before life and the healing now can fully be lived; 11) Emotional problems are good. Now that you've had time to let that become a part of your new way of thinking, I want to take the line of thought to another level. I want to try to convince you that emotional problems are good, that much can be gained from them; 12) Life is difficult. With the evidence all around us that life is difficult I'm amazed at how many of us refuse to accept this truth".[xiv]

Another very important concept to keeping an emotionally healthy life is that we reap what we sow. Whenever you do something negative, you're going to reap negative. Whenever you do something good, you're going to reap something good. Another important concept to helping a survivor keep emotionally healthy is to help the survivor manage stress. "Stress management is designed to teach individuals the power of choice and the consequences of poor choices. A combination of poor choices becomes a stress syndrome".[xv] Just as stress is the consequences of poor choice so is reaping what you sow. It is important to understand that what we do has a powerful affect on what is going to happen in the future.

One of the most important things that a survivor who has been ritually abused and has multiple personality disorder, is to be a part of the family. If a church or ministry is dealing with people that are S.R.A.M.P.D., it would be good for them to have a number of families in the community that would invite these people to go along with them to family events and treat them as part of their family. A lot of times people look at these people as being crazy or incompetent, when they are highly intelligent, wonderful, examples of human beings that need to be understood from the stand point of what they've been through and what God has for their life. Being a part of a family is something they are told when they are programmed they will never be a part of. They are told that any family will reject you, the church will reject you and Christians won't accept. So keeping emotional healthy in the healing process is not only being a part of a family but also knowing how to be a part of a family without being codependent and dependent on the ones that are ministering to the survivor. Another important point to remember that is in ritual abuse, there is a lot sexual abuse so there needs to be somebody or a couple of professionals that specialize in sexual abuse counseling to be able to come around the survivor and help them through some of the traumatic sexual experiences they have been through. It is important that the survivor is hooked into different agencies or with different Christian professionals who specialize in sexual abuse counseling.

The following are some key things we had to deal with in keeping a survivor emotionally healthy on a regular basis. The first thing we had to deal with was the problem of depression. Most often times after session, or after session where integration happened there would come a time or period where they would be depressed or feeling very much depressed, they would have new memories coming back to them, back to their minds, new thoughts, new feelings, and depression really was a huge part of the healing process, knowing how to deal with it. "Helping the depressed person, Dr. Lewis Jolyon West in his book, The Nature and Treatment of Depression, suggests four "R's" in helping the depressed person. 1) Rapport-it is very important that you establish rapport with the depressed person. The person needs to know that someone cares and is willing to take time to be concerned. 2) Reassurance-the depressed person also has a tremendous need for reassurance. Their tendency is to give up and they often need to be reassured again and again in a very calm manner. 3) Revelation-as a person talks with you, assist him in learning more about himself and the cause of the depression. 4) Reorganization-a depressed person should reorganize his life-style in some way. You may ask, "If you were not depressed, what would you do when you leave here today?" When the person has finished sharing these things, you could suggest that this is exactly what you would like him to do when he leaves". The second thing we dealt with on a regular basis and in a big way were thoughts of suicide. So often survivors deal with thoughts of suicide when going through the healing process. This is a very tricky part to deal with because if the survivor, when under your care, commits suicide, you could really be held liable so understand the warning signs and what to do for a suicidal person is very helpful. "Signs of the suicidal. A) Symptoms. A long serious illness can bring a person to the point of despair, especially if there is no hope at hand. B) Suicidal activity. There are many kinds of suicidal activity, which may be picked up by the observing counselor. They usually make sure that all the bills are paid, that the will is made out, and they have made arrangements just as though a person is going to take a long trip. C) Suicidal hint. Some individuals who have considered killing themselves are unclear in communicating that intent. They may make such statements as "you would be better off without me" or it's just that I hate to face each day". D) Suicidal threat. Any kind of suicide threat should be taken seriously. The majority of those who talk about suicide do attempt it at one time or another. E) Suicidal attempt. The suicidal attempt is a very clear and dramatic cry for help, and the person needs immediate help and support. Helping the suicidal person. Many people who are contemplating suicide will call a friend, a church, or an agency for assistance. If they call or you can see them face-to-face the following may be helpful in saving the person. A) Establish rapport and obtain information from the person. When the person calls or comes to see you, it is important to begin to develop a positive relationship. B) Seek to identify or clarify the problem. Hear the person's story with as few interruptions as possible. Encourage him to tell you what has let him to where he is presently. What is it that is bothering him now and what has he tried to do before to cope with his problem? Do not challenge his statements or say such things as, "Things are not as bad as they seem." Focus on what the person is feeling and assist them in clarifying those feelings. If he has difficulty expressing them, help him to label them. You can help him to express his overwhelming helplessness, which may be broken up into specific problems, and then you may offer solutions. When he can begin to see his problems he can begin to construct a specific plan for solving them". The third thing we dealt with quite often was demonic attacks and death grips that would come in the middle of the night and the survivor would call me choking and needing me to pray and to pray them through into victory. Basically it's at this point and times that we really depended on the blood and power of Christ to get the victory. Several times I prayed with survivors to get the victory in the name of Jesus. The fourth thing we dealt with a lot is astral projections. People who would be in ceremony during the night with the cult, their spirit would leave their body and come to the place where our survivor was and would be calling them to come out, come back to the cult, come back to the meeting or calling them to go to a place where they could pick them up and bring them back to meeting and try to continue to reprogram them. Astral projections, whether people believe in it or not, is a very real problem. Number five would be the fear of abduction. The survivor needs to know that they are in a safe place. This is very important for good mental health. This is a reality; they do abduct their members. We had a survivor get abducted and they took her to a place and put her on her knees and strapped her arms one to one side and one to the other, and put a strap around her neck and told her if she didn't renounce Christ they were going to burn her with an electric prod. They burnt her all over her back and then they said if she didn't renounce Christ they were going to kill her, and they raised a sacrificial knife up and she said when they did that, there came a bright light in the room and a robe and sandals were seen and the chords that they had tied around her were ripped and fell off. The reason I know this was true, she called me needing help, needed to come in and be treated. She came in and was treated for second and third degree burns from an electric prod that was all over her back and you could see the marks where they had her tied up and strapped her, so the fear of abduction is a very real thing. Number Six. Fear of hospitals. They are afraid of hospitals. They say the cult has members that are in hospitals and they are afraid that someone is going to come in and do a wrong treatment and that they would wind up dead. So they are really afraid of hospitals. Then there is the fear of rejection. That people won't believe their stories and that people won't accept them for who they are. One of the big things we found too, and also this is a key in keeping good mental health, because you don't want the work you're doing to be destroyed. So often a survivor, we had to keep the car keys from the survivor, the car, and everything, because other alters would come up that were cult loyal that would want to bring her to a meeting so that they could continue to reprogram what we were tearing apart. So, therefore, she had to really be watched and the car had to be chained to a tree and it got real ridiculous for a while. All these areas are important in keeping good mental health. The survivor needs to know that they are not condemned if they make a mistake and fail, they are not going to be rejected but that they are going to continue to be loved and that they will be continued to be worked with to bring them to healing and deliverance. Yet, it has to be stressed to the survivor that there are consequences to their choices and even though there are, they are still loved.

I can't stress this enough that if a church or ministry is going to deal with people who are S.R.A.M.P.D., that a team of people must be developed so that the survivor or survivors can be dealt with in an effective, healthy manner. And in that team needs to be churches, pastors, psychologists, psychiatrists, and I might add Christian psychologists and psychiatrists, and their time, if possible, needs to be donated as much as possible. There needs to be Christians who are trained at least in the basics of sitting and listening, confidential, who are willing to just sit and pray with the survivor. There needs to be a team approach and the thing is, dealing with this area is kind of a new thing in the body of Christ, but a team of people need to be developed and people need to share what they're learning with each other across the country so that we can minister to these people in the most effective way we can. And yet, if you have a team developed you're not going to be burnt out with the ministry. So the development of a team and a development of people who are skilled in the word of God, skilled in psychology, skilled in counseling people who are sexually abused, because when a team has been put together that can work

179

with these people on a weekly basis, on top of session work, then you can keep an emotionally healthy life.

# CHAPTER NINE

# IN CONCLUSION

In conclusion, I would like to say that I pray that this book has been a great help for those who are trying to bring survivors into healing. There is still so much to be learned and so much that needs to be discovered yet, in dealing with S.R.A.M.P.D., I can't stress enough that the only person that I know that could truly bring a survivor into total healing is the person of the Lord Jesus Christ. We are only servants, we are only conduits through which God can flow his power, and we are only cracked vessels, in which we hold the anointing of God. And my prayer is that those working with survivors, that God would give you wisdom, guidance and direction, and that this book would be help and an encouragement for those seeking to bring these last day warriors into healing. Because I believe, that once the survivors get healed up and the multiples get put back together, they're going to be some of the most powerful preachers and powerful people in the body of Christ that we have ever seen.

If you are reading this book and you don't know Jesus as your savior, I would like to invite you today to make Him Lord of your life. It does not matter what you think you've done or how bad of a sinner you think you are. You can be forgiven and set free. Just pray the following prayer. "Dear Jesus I believe you are the Son of God and that you died on the cross for me and on the third day you arose from the dead. I ask you today to forgive me of all my sins and come into my heart and be my Lord and Savior. Please teach me to live for you and what it means to be a Christian and fill me with the Holy Spirit in Jesus name I pray Amen."

If you prayed this prayer praise the Lord! Remember to read your Bible daily and ask the Holy Spirit to lead and guide you into all Truth and to a good church you can attend. I pray that this book has touched your heart and I give Jesus all the Glory!!

# CHAPTER TEN

# DEFINITION OF TERMS AND PHRASES

This chapter will be a definition of terms and phrases that would be good for the reader to understand and know before you read the work. These are common terms and phrases that are used when dealing with someone that wants to come into healing, someone who has been through ritual abuse and someone who has multiple personality disorder. The following are the terms and phrases:

1.  Altar-this is a table that is used to hold artifacts during rituals. It may be made up of wood, earth or stone.

2. Alter personality or alter-this is a distinct and separate personality with different values and a different range of emotions and a history of its own experiences within the same person.

3. Anointing-this is a Christian term used to refer to the power of the Holy Spirit acting through them in a special or in an unusual way or an unusual situations. This special power enables a believer to be particularly effective or insightful in a variety of areas of ministry.

4. Astral projection-this happens when a person's spirit is traveling outside of the natural body and many times it goes great distances and on different planes of consciousness.

5. Binding or rebuking evil spirits-this is using the power and authority in the name of Jesus Christ according to Matthew 18:18-20, to bind Satan in Jesus' name and rebuke evil spirits through the power of His name and His blood because the Lord has given us His authority. Luke 9:1, "when Jesus had called the twelve together He gave them power and authority to drive out all demons and to cure diseases and He sent them out to preach the kingdom of God and to heal the sick".

6. Birth person-this is the core part of the person who is born. This person has memories all the way back to the womb and may or may not be the same as the original person.

7.  Core-this is a personality that has memories back to the womb.

8.  Core split-this is a personality that has been split directly from the core.

9.  Crack person-this is an alter personality that was split but never was programmed or traumatized in any way and has kind of like fallen between the cracks of the system with no name and no assignment. These are also the alter personalities that are used in program to take the place of other systems that have gone to be with Jesus.

10. Cult alters-these are alter personalities who participate in cult activities. They could ultimately be serving a protective purpose due to brainwashing; they may become cult loyal to various degrees. When a survivor is coming into healing and has accepted Christ, there still may be some alters within them that are still cult loyal.

11. Demon-this is an evil spirit.

12. Demonization-this is varying degrees of demonic influence or control over a person's life or over an alter personality.

13. Disassociation-this is a process of separating from an event or an experience. Everyone has some ability to disassociate.

14. Dissociative identity disorder-other wise known as DID-this is the new official term known for multiple personality disorder.

15. False christ-this is a spirit that comes during session which a multiple can also see on the inside, this is a spirit claiming to be Christ but it is really a demon masquerading as a angel of light.

16. Host personality-this is the particular personality who is out most of the time and usually doesn't remember most of the abuse and alter personalities in the beginning of treatment. The particular role of the host is to carry out and to carry on with the daily routine of life and to fit into society.

17. Integration-this is where two or more alter personalities merge together to form a single personality. The new rejoined personality will retain the experiences and memories of the previously separated personalities.

18. Little ones-little ones are alter personalities who have been split who do not remember very much, who aren't very old and they haven't been programmed, they haven't been traumatized, and they often come in groups and they like to come out and talk and they like to go to Jesus and they don't really have any vows to break and they integrate real easy.

19. Loss of time-this happens to the host when another personality comes out and the host is not aware of it, so

when the host comes back out, maybe an hour or two or three hours has elapsed and they don't know what happened during that time period.

20. Multiple-this is a person with one or more personalities within the same person.  This is also someone who has been diagnosed with Dissociative identity disorder (DID).

21. Program-this is a predetermined response pattern established in a person's mind which happens automatically when triggered by a certain stimulus.

22. Programming-this is a predetermined response pattern deliberately put in a person's mind through mind control techniques into lower levels of the consciousness to direct their behavior, thoughts, emotions or withholding of information.

23. Ritual abuse-this is a methodical form of abuse or a systematic form of abuse usually with a predetermined purpose or agenda.

24. Satanic cult-this is a very organized group of people with an established belief system involving the direct worship of Satan or the demons in seeking and exercising of occult powers.

25. Satanic ritual abuse-otherwise known as S.R.A.-this happens when severe trauma or torture is experienced at the hand of a satanic cult to deliberately cause disassociation in a person so that they will develop multiple personalities so that those personalities can be

indoctrinated, programmed and demonized, bringing that individual under the control of the cult and kingdom of darkness, generally without the knowledge of the host personality.

26. Seeing on the inside-someone who has multiple personalities can see on the inside just like we can see on the outside; the inside will have landscaping, they will be able to see the other personalities, they will be able to see Jesus coming to them, they can hear things on the inside and hear others talk; their world on the inside is just as real as the world on the outside.

27. Spiritual warfare-this is the putting into action of spiritual principles which apply the authority of Christ and the blood of Jesus and the power of the Holy Spirit to come against demonic activity.

28. Split-this is the form alter personalities through disassociation.

29. Survivor-this is a person who has been severely abused who could also be referred to as a victim or survivor.

30. Switching-this is the process of changing control of the body from one personality to another personality.

31. System-this is a group of alter personalities, then one individual who are orgnized into a distinct system to have a distinct authority and structure that functions more or less independently within the whole.

**32.** **Trigger-this is a particular stimulus that will cause a response or put a program into action.**

# ENDNOTES

i "Uncovering The Mystery Of M.P.D.", Dr. James G. Friesen.

ii 8 "Power Healing", Rev. John Wimber

iii 11 "Care-Giving The Cornerstone of Healing", Cheryl S. Knight, M.S., CSW and Jo M. Getzinger, ACSW, CCSW.

iv 12 "Care-Giving The Cornerstone of Healing", Cheryl S. Knight, M.S., CSW and Jo M. Getzinger, ACSW, CCSW.

18 "The Three Battle Grounds", Francis Frangipane.

v 21 "The Final Quests", Rick Joyner.

vi 22 "Miracle Results Of Fasting", Dave Williams.

vii 36 King James Version, American Bicentennial 2nd Edition

41 "Care-Giving The Cornerstone of Healing", Cheryl S. Knight, M.S., CSW and Jo M. Getzinger, ACSW, CCSW.

43 "Exorcism Fact or Fiction?", Dr. Ken Olsen.

viii 44 "Restoring Shattered Lives", Dr. Tom Hawkins.

ix 45 "Dynamics of Faith", Carolina University of Theology.

x 46 Quotes by Pastor Jim Casey.

xi 47 "Journey to Wholeness", Carolina University of Theology.

xii 48 "Care-Giving The Cornerstone of Healing", Cheryl S. Knight, M.S., CSW and Jo M. Getzinger, ACSW, CCSW.

49 S.R.A. #2-Quote by Julie.

50 "Care-Giving The Cornerstone of Healing", Cheryl S. Knight, M.S., CSW and Jo M. Getzinger, ACSW, CCSW.

51 S.R.A. #2-Quote by Sharon.

52 CP-609, "Cognitive Therapy Techniques In Christian Counseling", Carolina University of Theology.

53 "Effective Biblical Counseling", Lawrence J. Crabb Jr.

68 S.R.A. #1-Quote by Julie.

70 "Bibles Answers to Man's Questions on Demons", Kenneth E. Hagin, Volume 4 of the Satan, Demons, and Demon Possession Series.

xiii 71 CP-612, "Crisis Counseling-Turning Points", Carolina University of Theology.

xiv

# BIBLIOGRAPHY

1. N.I.V. Study Bible, Zondervan Publishing House, Grand Rapids, MI, 49530, General Editor Kenneth Barker, Associate Editors Donald Burdick, John Stek, Walter Wessel, and Ronald Youngblood.

2. Survivor's Testimonies: 1, 2, and 3 names and addresses cannot be released for the privacy of the survivors. Thanks to the three survivors for their work for this book.Three Dimensional Black Widow Programming.

3. Pastor Jim Casey. A Pastor who has worked several years helping people to leave Satanism and helping hurting people in counseling.

4. C.A.R.E., Inc., 3069 South M-37, Baldwin, MI 49034, Jo Getzinger and Cheryl Night, M.S., CSW, (616) 745-0500.

5. "Power Healing", Rev. John Wimber, Harper Collins.

6. Restoration In Christ Ministries, Dr. Tom Hawkins, P.O. Box 479, Grottoes, VA, 24441-0479, (540) 298-2272.

7. "The Final Quests", Rick Joyner, Morning Star Publications, P.O. Box 369, Pineville, SC, 28134: pgs. 53-56.

8. "Miracle Results of Fasting", David Williams, Decapolis Publishing, 1997, pgs. 71.

9. "Satanic Ritual Abuse and Secret Societies" Video, David Carrico, 1995, (90 min.).

10. "The Legend of the Phoenix", Elon College, North Carolina, 2700 Campus Box, Elon College, NC, 27244-2010, E-Mail: web@elon.edu, 1-800-334-8448.

11. "Apostolic Realities, The Principalities and Powers", Art Katz, http://beinsrael.org/index.html.

12. "Diagnostic and Statistical manual of Mental Disorders" (DSM IV).  This manual is used by Mental Health Professionals for the classification, definition and standardization of terminology in this field.

13. "Counseling Toward Wholeness", Dr. D. Clifton Wood, The Wesley Press, Marion, IN 46952.

14. "Effective Biblical Counseling", Lawrence J. Crabb, Jr., Library of Congress Cataloging in Publication Data.

15. "Bible Answers to Mans Questions on Demons", Kenneth E. Hagin Ministries, P.O. Box 50126, Tulsa, OK, 74150.

16. "Exorcism Fact or Fiction", Dr. Ken Olsen, Thomas Nelson Publishers, 1992.

17. "The 12 Best Kept Secrets For Living An Emotionally Healthy Life", Dr. Chris Thurman, Thomas Nelson, Inc., Nashville, TN, 1993.

18. "Unbroken Curses", Rebecca Brown, M.D. with Daniel Yoder, Whitaker House, 580 Pittsburgh Street, Springdale, PA, 15144.

19. "Uncovering The Mystery of M.P.D.", James G. Friesen, Here's Life Publishers, Inc., San Bernandino, CA, 1991.

20. "The Three Battle Grounds", Francis Frangipane, Arrow Publications, P.O. Box 10102, Cedar Rapids, IA, 52410, November 1989.

21. "Resolving DID", Tom R. Hawkins, Ph.D., Restoration In Christ Ministries, P.O. Box 479, Grottoes, VA, 24441-0479, 1997, 2000.

22. "Stress: The Inevitable Peace: The Possibility", Dr. William F. Lee, 213 Edinboro Dr., Southern Pines, NC, 28387, 1989.

23. "Dynamics Of Faith", Carolina University of Theology, CP-608, Gods Way to Move Mountains.

24. "Cognitive Therapy Techniques In Christian Counseling", Carolina University of Theology, CP-609, Mark R. McMinn, Ph.D.

25. "Restoring The Foundations Counseling By The Living Word", Chester and Betsy Kylstra, Pub. Proclaiming His Word, P.O. Box 2339, Santa Rosa Beach, FL, 32459, 1994, 1996, All Rights Reserved.

26. "Turning Points", Carolina University of Theology, CP-612.

27. "Journey To Wholeness", Carolina University of Theology, CP-607, And Foreword By: Dr. Stan DeKoven.

28. King James Version Bible, American Bicentennial 2nd Edition, Jerry Falwell Ministries, Lynchburg, VA, 24514, Published By, Thomas Nelson Publishing, Inc., Nashville, TN, USA, 1964

# ABOUT THE AUTHOR

John Clark has a B.A. in Religion from Bethany Bible College from Sussex, New Brunswick, Canada, M.A. and Ph. D in Christian counseling Psychology from Carolina University of Theology in Stanley North Carolina. He is a member of The American Society of Christian Therapist at the Doctoral level. He has nine years of Pastoral experience and six years of experience as a Hospital Chaplain and has worked over 500 Hours with S.R.A.M.P.D., and John Clark and his wife help oversee the Healing and Deliverance Ministry for their local Church.